BODYBUILDERS NEVER DIE:
THEY SIMPLY LOSE THEIR PUMP

BODYBUILDERS NEVER DIE:
THEY SIMPLY LOSE THEIR PUMP

JIM MOORE

Pitch Publishing
A2 Yeoman Gate
Yeoman Way
Durrington
BN13 3QZ
www.pitchpublishing.co.uk

© Jim Moore, 2013

A CIP catalogue record is available for this book
from the British Library

ISBN-13: 978-1-90917-882-3

Typesetting and origination by Pitch Publishing.
Printed and bound by CPI Group (UK) Ltd, Croydon, CR0 4YY

Contents

Dedicated to the memories of

Mum and Dad:

"Apple" Annie and

"Rory" Norman Moore

and also to Jo for sharing my

life, my love, my heart.

Bodybuilders never die – they simply lose their pump

I NEVER started out to write a story, but when you are going stir crazy at home and the doctors are telling you non-stop to rest, I thought that I would risk exercising the only two digits that I can type with. If you're looking for an exercise or drug manual, then this isn't for you. This is a personal account of a journey, and if you're not an Iron Warrior, then I think it will give you a unique, no bullshit insight into what it takes to create a world-class physique and if you are one of the brethren, then maybe you will know someone like me or perhaps you'll see yourself in my words.

Apart from the celebrated years of Arnold and films like *Pumping Iron*, bodybuilding is a much marginalised sport. In fact, when it is shown in the mainstream media, it is often in derogatory terms as some kind of homoerotica or they get some poor twat and poke fun at him. The only time bodybuilding is ever taken seriously is when it is demonised as in the case of people like Greg Valentino who used a drug called Synthol to make his arms look freaky, or Beryl "Beef It" Fox who murdered his wife.

I have spent most of my life trying to defend my sport and I have realised that the bodybuilding magazines only ever highlight a handful of top bodybuilders with their glamorous lifestyles and people have very little insight into the bread and butter competitors like me. People have even asked me how much money I have made in winning my five titles. I think they are shocked when I tell them that I had won very little money and apart from some sponsorship, competing for nearly 20 years had cost me a small fortune.

My story is far from glamorous, but it isn't ugly either. It is full of true-life events that I hope will tell you just how dedicated all the guys and girls who compete are. I will tell you how from my humble beginning of training in a makeshift gym at home, I ended up on stage competing against the best athletes in the world.

Hopefully people will see that bodybuilding is a lot more that just drugs; it takes dedication and guts and a lot of knowledge, with a little bit of insanity thrown in for good measure! Go past any gym in the morning or late at night – and I am not talking about leisure clubs here, where many of the so-called beautiful people go through the motions of training because they fear if they grimaced, they would need to take another visit to the local Botox clinic. No, I am talking about real gyms, where the screams of pain can be heard and the smell of sweat and Ralgex greets you on arrival. No matter what time of year, rain, snow or sunshine, you'll see them, the dedicated either smashing out reps or torturing themselves on the bike or stepper machines.

I have collapsed many times in the gym, had nosebleeds, thrown up during workouts. To me and, as the world would describe them, the other "fanatics", this was accepted as an everyday occurrence as we drove ourselves through session after session of masochistic intensity in pursuit of our dreams. I will take you into a world where the word average is spat out with distaste; I will speak of the drugs, the crazy and often humorous situations that I found myself in. I will introduce you to the people who shared my life, some dodgy as hell, some sadly no longer with us, but what we had in common was our love of the iron.

This is the journey I took to turn a wiry, long distance runner's body of eight stone into a ripped up championship frame of over 15 stone. I will talk of victory, overcoming adversity and the drive and passion that made me into a world-class physique, but ultimately nearly killed me.

My introduction to the iron

THE PHYSIQUE is created for many reasons; some to keep the outside world at bay, some in the vain pursuit of attracting women, some in the hope of feeling "loved". For others like me it was a mixture of all three and the ultimate stage to display it on: The Bodybuilding Competition. A place where one is judged not on strength but on the look of the physique. Its ideals are to show maximum muscularity with minimum body fat.

I never set out to be a bodybuilder. I certainly never thought that I would compete, let alone be fairly successful, in fact I think you could call me a bodybuilder by accident, but let's get on with the story.

I am a competitive bastard. It wouldn't matter if it was Monopoly or Tiddlywinks, I would do anything to win, but it wasn't always that way. In fact as a kid, I was darn right lazy. My first introduction to weights was when after much prompting and the bribe of buying me some sweets after, I got on the bus one night with my bro to an old terraced house in Manchester. The guy's name was Harry and he had turned the main bedroom of his house into a small gym. I often wonder nowadays how he managed to convince his poor long-suffering wife that utilising their best bedroom and no doubt demoting her to one of the smaller rooms was a good idea. He seemed quite old but at the age of ten, I guess anyone over 30 was ancient.

Rumour had it that he was an accomplished strongman until his left arm was run over by a steam engine. I remember trying to get a glimpse of his arm to see if it was actually flat like something out of a cartoon, but much to my disappointment, his arm seemed relatively normal. His chest on the other hand seemed huge; much exacerbated no doubt by his habit of inflating his chest muscles whenever he talked to you.

The room was stark and cold, filled with a bench press, squat stands and various plates and bars. I can remember our kid gasping with the effort as he worked his socks off, while I watched and wondered what all the commotion was about, no doubt dreaming of the treat that I would get for going.

If I wasn't there, I would be swimming. My dad loved the baths and I on the other hand didn't. I could cope with the swimming, but having to walk three miles home shivering against the cold rain was a total bitch. In fact Dad was into anything sporty, he was a decent boxer and a very good swimmer, even at a height of 5ft 4in. He had once held the combined Forces all-comers backstroke record. Our back yard was used for everything; shot put, long jump, high jump and he even made some old wooden stakes to represent hurdles to practise with.

Football was what I loved though. If you asked kids of my age what they wanted to be, most would have replied: "Georgie Best!" He was my first and many of the other kids' idol. We all wanted to be able to dribble like George, therefore most games were full of strikers. No one wanted to be a full-back or midfielder so if someone had a football we would either play out in the street until the neighbours moved us on or spend hours in the local park, sometimes until it was so dark you could hardly make out where the ball was.

Running was what I did most. Back then, in an avenue with over 100 houses, there was only one family with a car. I think they were called Jones, proper posh they were or so we thought. It wasn't just at the athletic club, I ran everywhere – to school, back for dinner, back to school, well until I was 14 and then I seemed to develop some kind of amnesia and although I set out for school, I often ended up in the centre of Manchester where most of the other truants congregated.

I don't know where the laid-back personality that I had went but I guess it got thrown out with puberty. Suddenly everything I did was a competition; it didn't matter if it was chess, I wanted to win. I was a decathlete long before it became trendy, not in the sense of Daley Thompson, but I immersed myself into all sports – long and high jump, shot put, javelin and discus: sprinting, long distance and even swimming which I was crap at.

What I lacked in skill I tried to make up with sheer determination. If someone could do 50 press-ups I had to do 60 or die trying and I am not just saying that as a throwaway word, I literally would drive myself through pain to win. I had some success in other sports, but now I realise that my obsessive, driven nature was like a sculpture awaiting form and that the sport of bodybuilding was there to feed my need for self-determination.

So you can see, even though my family were into sport, I wasn't brought up with the media images of Stallone, Van Damme or Schwarzenegger that young people are exposed to today. Our ideas of what a muscular physique should look like were from advertisements in magazines and comics displaying Charles Atlas, who was probably the most famous strongman back in those days, flexing his muscles and stating how the latest home gadget had transformed his body overnight.

One of the fads at the time was the Bullworker, it was highly marketed and the hype behind it promised much success. We, like many homes had one. In fact I think it was my brother Chris who bought it. Like most other people who used them, for the first few weeks we would all try to out-do each other, taking turns in front of the mirror, trying to copy the exercises. I used to take my top off in my bedroom and attack the Bullworker with all the aggression and determination I could muster but the damn thing refused to budge even an inch and I would always end up on the bed sweaty, gasping for breath and defeated.

I don't think it was any surprise that eventually, after becoming a dust-stopper for many months, ours ended up in the dustbin like most of the others that had been bought on the back of good intentions.

So any thoughts of bodybuilding were light years from my mind after my earlier exposure to the sport. My memories of training at Harry's coupled with the non-movement of the Bullworker hadn't really inspired me. In fact I thought it was downright boring and I never had an inkling that one day it would be such a huge part of my life.

I was a runner, not a great one though. My idols were Steve Ovett and Sebastian Coe, two of the greatest middle-distance runners Britain ever produced. What I lacked in ability I doggedly made up for in guts, but I was far from having the beautiful silky gliding style of the top stars. Every week I was doing over 80 miles of running. It was the time before jogging became cool and my training runs would often be accompanied by shouts of abuse from people or the odd stray dog trying to bite my arse.

But it's strange how things happen though isn't it? There I was – this young guy minding his own business, fairly happy with life, although I must admit at times, I resented the fact that I looked so skinny, but runners, unless they are sprinters, seldom look muscular. Anyway, my own love affair with bodybuilding started while I was nursing an injury to my right knee caused by too much running on roads. I had to rest up and to relieve the monotony, I happened to wander into the local library on a fairly dull and uninspiring afternoon.

I was looking for a book by the aforementioned Mr Ovett and began browsing through the autobiographies when fate intervened and changed my life completely. I came across this rather insignificant book that blended into the lines of other literature. It was the name that attracted me. I had heard it before from the film *Pumping Iron* which I think was the only film about bodybuilding that had been circulated to the general public. The first thing I noticed was the cover; it displayed this handsome muscular tanned guy, looking the epitome of health. The book was called *Education Of A Bodybuilder*. It was the story of one of the greats of the sport: Arnold Schwarzenegger.

I ended up taking it home among several other books that I had chosen but that night, I decided to read it first. It drew me into its story. I could identify with its author, I was engrossed by how he had once been a slim young man and how through training with weights, he had built his body to become the world champion. He stated how bodybuilding had made him more confident and how it had opened the doors to fortune, fame and girls. The book endorsed this by depicting photos of him surrounded by beautiful women. By the end of the book, I was a disciple!

But unfortunately I was a disciple without the means, I didn't have any weights at home at the time and I certainly hadn't got the confidence to show my scrawny body in a gym but my birthday was coming up and after I had harangued my family about the virtues of bodybuilding to the point that I think they started to avoid me. More in an attempt to stop me going on about it all the time than anything, my brother finally gave in and bought me a Weider weight training kit. It had dumbbells and a barbell and the weight was 100lb. It wasn't made of iron though, it was garish blue and plastic. I had no benches, no squat stands and to be honest not much idea either. All I knew was that Arnold had used weights to fashion his massive muscular frame and this was admired by women and that was good enough for me.

I set everything up in the spare room and religiously studied the exercise diagrams and started a three-day weekly programme that split the physique up into three body parts. I contorted my skinny body, trying to emulate the poses of the guys on the charts, my ribs sticking out where muscles should have been, but my eight-stone wet through body had taken its first faltering steps on the road to muscle madness.

Three days a week I would seclude myself away pumping the iron. My weedy frame would scream out the exercises as though my life depended on it. I now detested the image that represented me, and used the self hate to drive me on. I never missed a work-out and those few weights that lay in the spare room became beacons of hope that would help me escape from how I felt about myself.

What I didn't know at the time was that no matter what size I was, I would still experience the same loathing. My idea of a diet those days was fish fingers and chips, bacon and tinned tomatoes with loads of white bread and anything else that was being cooked for dinner, but my metabolism was so fast that at the end of two years of training I might have hardly looked a stereotypical bodybuilder. In fact I still looked like the proverbial guy who has sand kicked in his face, but now the scales read 10st 7lbs and to me that was all that mattered.

I began to understand that the guys with the really big physiques used equipment and machines like leg presses and the home-made bench that I had now made and the few vinyl blue weights were not going to give me the body I wanted. According to the bodybuilding bibles of which

I was now a staunch follower, if I wanted to fulfil my physique to its maximum potential, I would have to go to a gym.

There were only a few gyms in Warrington. I first thought of using the fitness suite at the baths, but the predicates of iron stated with derisive undertones that these places were not for true iron brethren. It was around this time that my father had met a man called Walter O'Malley in the local bookmakers, who unbeknown to either of us was a former Mr Universe. He told my father that I should come down to his gym as training at home would only take me so far.

I felt confident that my new "beefed up" frame would be okay in such surroundings until I approached the black gates of the gym and saw these huge guys coming out wearing shorts and tank tops, their swelling muscles bulging and walking the walk that said "don't mess with me".

I slithered past them, faltering and dithering, before finally summoning the courage to open the door. The smell of Ralgex was the first thing that hit me and then the line of muscular guys sat around the reception area. I could sense the chant of "new meat, new meat!" I felt like the biblical Christian about to be thrown to the lions.

The girl behind the counter looked up from filing her nails and stared at me too. The distance to the counter had now magnified to at least a mile, my legs felt like they had done a workout already as I felt them wobbling like jelly. I finally got in front of the counter and I heard someone shout: "I've never seen a lat move before." My paranoia by this point was compounded by the girl on reception asking me if I wanted the fitness centre down the road. I could see her looking me up and down and all I could think was: "Do I look that out of place?" I sneaked a look at the muscle-heads and thought: "Maybe I do, where is this fitness centre?" But the words of iron gurus echoed in my head that if I wanted to get bigger, this was the place to be.

I couldn't look at her as my voice quivered, but I confirmed that I wanted to pay for a casual workout. I quickly paid the money that she asked for and I sought the refuge of the changing room, thinking that would help me escape the glares of the muscular beasts camped in reception. The changing rooms were empty and I breathed a sigh of relief as I donned my medium-sized t-shirt and tracksuit bottoms. I could hear the clanging of the weights accompanied by screams as though people were being tortured even before I opened the door of the changing rooms.

The weight room was like another world. It was crowded and the smell of testosterone-fuelled energy with overtones of outright violence seemed to escape from every beast that was either screaming out reps or pacing menacingly up and down psyching themselves up to lift these huge columns of iron.

Seeing them clothed in their baggies and cut-down vests, I felt like I had walked into another world. Even the language was different; wheels I learnt were your legs and guns your arms. I was in awe of the huge racks of dumbbells that had weights that looked more like thick sets of wheels and at the end, a black pair of boulders sagged into the iron structure that held them and etched across each of them was the daunting figure of 160lb. All I could think was "that's much more than I weigh in a single dumbbell" and I was suddenly stunned back into reality as this muscular black guy pushed past me and grabbed them and then started to heave them into the air above his chest. All around me were exercise stations with massive brick-shaped weights.

For some people this would have been enough and they would have looked for the nearest escape route. Indeed, I did look at the fire escape and I could hear the theme music from the film *The Great Escape* being played in my head, but despite feeling nervous, I found myself looking around with a big smile on my face and thinking: "I want to look like these guys!"

Four days a week I would run the gauntlet of the reception filled with over-sized muscle-heads. By this time I was drawing attention as the skinny guy who fought for every rep. I couldn't compete with their muscle, but what I lacked in size and strength I made up with sheer determination. I never made much eye contact as the place still resembled a post-apocalyptic world filled with over-sized human beings whose main conversations when they weren't grunting were of inflicting serious injuries to members of the non-lifting public.

I never missed a workout; I would push my body so hard that I would come off the bench press with my lip bleeding where I had bit into it. I was surrounded by people doing the same and the atmosphere was charged with raw aggression and in my mind when I lifted, I attacked it like my life depended on it. This is how the guys with the huge physiques trained, so this was my approach too.

After a few months, the reception area no longer seemed like the induction wing of a prison. I would get the odd nod or smile as I walked in, and some would even stop and offer advice. I remember once when I was doing wide grip bench presses that worked my pectoral muscles or pecs as they are also known. I was on my own, giving it everything as usual and went for the extra rep, but as it came down, my arms were shaking. I could feel the weight descending and then it happened; my strength went completely and it got stuck across my chest. Now this is an embarrassing situation nearly every bodybuilder has faced and the dilemma is this: Do you shout like hell for help? Do you let it lie across your chest and take a few minutes to rest, then try again? Or do you try to roll the bar down your body, manoeuvre it over your belt and risk ruining your wedding tackle?

I opted for the lie there and hope I could eventually press the weight up again. I could feel it digging into my chest, affecting my breathing, but I summoned up everything I had and pushed. The bar rose a few inches and fell again across my chest as quickly as a magnet attracting iron filings. I was stuck, I lay there contemplating whether to try to roll the bar down and escape like that, but I was interrupted by a voice saying "here pal let me help you with that" as he took the bar off me with infinite ease.

It was only when I stood up to say thanks that I realised it was Frank, who was a top pro in his time. He looked huge and I felt embarrassed that he had to help me, but he just smiled and said: "You don't give up do you?" as he moved away and carried on with his own training.

I would look around me and see the guys grunting and screaming as they tortured their muscles into new growth and then use it as my motivation. I trained and fought through endless workouts. I wasn't as big as most of the people, but it didn't stop me from giving everything I had. The gym was becoming my home, it was a place I could ditch whatever other problems I had and it promised salvation, a chance to rid myself of the skinny reflection that stared back at me in the mirror and replace it with a body I could be happy with.

I didn't realise it at the time but I was beginning to experience the disease that most bodybuilders suffer from. The guys call it Bigorexia, but its real name is body dysmorphia. The syndrome is the reverse of anorexia – people who have it see themselves as smaller than they actually are. It's a doubled-edged sword for many bodybuilders. It means that many of us are never satisfied and constantly strive to gain more muscle but the downside to it means many often take greater and greater risks to try to attain the huge physiques that they feel they need.

During this time I started work at Warrington boxing club as a general assistant. I would teach circuit training to the guys and I also got involved in the conditioning work. The first time I met Jay he squeezed himself through the frame of the door. I was told he was a top ABA heavyweight boxer in his time but the drink and some petty criminal offences had stopped his career.

He wasn't greatly muscled in a bodybuilding sense but I had seen him at O'Malley's gym heaving massive amounts of iron and now on the heavy bag. He made it wince and crumple with every punch he threw. After about an hour he came over to chat to me and said he had seen me at the gym. He said the guys were impressed that I trained so hard and he said I could train with him if I wanted. Jay was legendary in Warrington for his sheer strength and the fact that even if he missed with a punch, people would be "downed" by the backdraft. So it was with a mixture of excitement and fear that I agreed to meet him the next day for a "back" workout.

After meeting Jay in the reception area of O'Malley's, we entered the arena of the weights room and he chatted about how he had got weaker as he was getting older, but as he sat down at the lateral pull down machine and he started his "warm-up" poundage, I began to realise just how strong he was. His "warm-up" was heavier than I could use but train we did and I never gave up on any rep, always fighting for that last inch of movement.

After the lat pull-downs we went on to t-bar rows and again he started to heave huge poundages, then we had to strip the bar down for my set. I thought this would make Jay a bit fed up but he said he liked the way I gave everything every set and he had trained with strong guys who just played at training, but I made him train with intensity. After the workout he bought us both a protein shake and he explained that we have to restore our bodies with carbs and proteins as he sank a double MetRX protein shake.

By now and probably because I was training with Jay, the banter was friendlier and I began to feel accepted by the guys. They were definitely a bunch of lads that you wouldn't walk down a back alley and meet. Paul, the black guy that I had seen on my first visit hoisting the 160 dumbbells, stood well over 6ft 3in tall and his back was so wide that if he ever tried to commit suicide by jumping out of a window, he would float back gently to earth. His job, he told me, was as a crowd control technician, which meant he stood on the door of the local nightclub and excluded socially unacceptable people from entering or assisted them to leave in a most unfriendly way. In other words, he was a "bouncer".

So in fact were most of the other guys. They used the day to train and eat to get as huge and strong as possible to assist them with their night-time vocation. Robby was one too. He was most distinguished as he had two large circular earrings dangling from each ear which complemented his Mohawk haircut and the myriad of tattoos that adorned his massive body. Robby rarely spoke, in fact it was over a year until he accepted me socially. I felt a strange mixture of fear and trepidation when we met on the gang walk into the gym. He looked at me with a stare that never moved and then he nodded his head at me in a welcoming gesture. I now knew I had been totally accepted, I was now a "bodybuilder".

I was told by the other guys that on many occasions they had more trouble trying to restrain Robby from going over the top when a rumble started at the club. Rob would bite and beat club-goers to a pulp if the other guys didn't intervene. You could tell when Robby was sat on his favourite bench in the market square because the crowds of people would make a diversion around him.

Andy was a lot smaller but had a much more defined build. He wasn't over the top in a muscular way but he was a good boxer who had fought some of the country's leading contenders. All the guys respected him and he was the leading doorman at the club too. He also used to come into the boxing club where I worked and I was very wary of him at first because he had a reputation that preceded him. He was also a ladies' man and had an entourage of women that he treated like a conveyor belt. He was front of house at the club and with his good looks and physique, the supply of ladies was endless.

Andy might have been dwarfed by the other doormen, but he was one hell of a fighter and in any fracas was often the first guy at the scene of any trouble. He didn't fight dirty, he would try to talk them out the club and if this didn't work then he would knock them out. We used to all mess around and have impromptu boxing sessions at the club. You would don the head guard and get the sparring gloves on that were huge and resembled mini pillows, but I never saw anyone in the ring with either Andy or Jay. Most of the lads were young, headstrong and some even a little crazy, but no one was certifiable or that partial to hospital food.

The boxing gym had many characters. Bob, for instance, had been one of the leading exponents of martial arts in his time, but he had gone to "seed" and he was now definitely over his fighting weight. In fact he had a gut, but most of the young guys that he sparred with were shocked how when he got in the ring with them, he metamorphosed into a fast and deadly opponent.

His pet hate, like a lot of the lads, was arrogance. I recall on one occasion, another guy who practised karate had been "teaching" this young kid with learning disabilities how to fight. A few of us had heard this lad scream and whimper and we rushed through to see what was wrong as it was obvious by the noise that someone was hurt. It was a sickening sight that met our eyes; this poor kid was cowering while "Mr Karate" was circling him like a lion surveying its prey. I shouted: "What the fuck are you doing?" and Mr Karate said: "Teaching him some moves!"

A few of us got into the ring to rescue the young guy; his legs were bruised and swollen, where this idiot had used him for target practice. The kid was jittery and really shaken. I was fucking fuming as I led the kid away and took him downstairs to get some ice to try to stop the swelling. Eventually after he seemed a little calmer, I walked him home. His mother was furious. The kid had come to our club to develop some confidence and although the guys included him in some good-natured banter, there was no malice and he had grown in confidence over the weeks he had been coming in and now after this incident, she feared he might not come ever again.

I gave my re-assurance that I would talk to Trevor, the manager, and get him banned. I was pissed off with myself as I walked back to the club; I felt that I should have been more vigilant. I was just filling Trevor in about what had happened earlier, he was taking one of the boxing sessions, when the gym door crashed open and the kid's mum swept in, teary-eyed and bursting with anger and emotion as she spat out words of venom. She told the whole room what this piece of garbage had done to her son.

After Trevor had eventually calmed her down and took her to his office, I tried to restart the session, but now the atmosphere had turned from hard graft to sheer anger. Most of the guys knew the kid with learning disabilities but to be honest, it wasn't so much that he had been hurt, it was that most of the guys hated the idiot that had done it and now it was the Mr Karate that I felt sorry for. He had stirred up a hornets' nest of people who had more than enough talent to give a real good hiding.

Fortunately for him, it was Bob that got to him first. I say fortunate because Bob was a gentleman and it took a lot to anger or get him roused. Some of the others wanted to kill him and I had no doubt in my mind that if they had seen him, they would have. I will never forget the guy's face when he cockily strutted into the gym; I mean, he was a black belt, so he must have been fairly useful. If he hadn't been so arrogant, he would have sensed that all was not well.

I was sweeping up as he nodded to me as though nothing had happened and he went into the changing rooms. A few of the guys stopped their work and started to walk to the back room where he was getting changed, when Bob just said quietly: "Sorry boys he's mine!" Mr Karate came walking back in at that moment, dressed in his gi complete with his black belt. Bob just calmly walked up to him and said: "I believe you need someone to spar with?" He laughed and said: "Any time pal." "That's good, I'll go and get changed," replied Bob. I must admit this guy looked fast as he was warming up and I although knew about Bob's background, I thought maybe he had bitten off more than he could chew. I needn't have worried.

It was almost comical when they climbed into the ring. The people who were in the gym gathered around like a lynch mob. It was like a scene from the western *High Noon*. This guy was punching the air and looking aggressively at Bob and he just strolled to the centre of the ring like it was a Sunday morning and he was going to read the papers. They touched gloves and this guy came right at Bob with a kick to his head and then it happened. Bob just caught his foot and in one fluid blurring motion the guy was on his back. Bob gestured for him to get back up and the guy was raging and came at Bob with left and right combinations, but he just blocked the punches, and somehow he bent the guy's arm at the same time and sent an open-handed chop to the guy's neck and he just fell to the floor as if he had been shot.

He then staggered back up and aimed another kick at Bob and once again, he blocked it as though he was having a picnic out there and then sent his own devastating kick to the guy's groin. The piercing scream the guy made filled the gym and the crowd of people were all laughing, baying for blood, but Bob just bowed, then leant over him and said in a voice not much than a whisper: "We don't have bullies in here, you're banned."

He eventually got to his feet and to as torrent of threats and abuse he left the gym in disgrace.

It was hard to digest what I had seen. Portly Bob had turned into this devastating vigilante in front of my eyes and now the deed had been done, he just shrugged off the back-slapping, picked up his paper and went about picking out his horses that he was backing. It seriously was like watching Clark Kent turn into Superman with not a telephone kiosk in sight.

Getting the needle

B Y THE time 1994 had raised its weary head, I had trained and socialised with the guys for about six years and it had become apparent that although I trained as hard as them and I had developed more knowledge of nutrition, that their extreme physiques weren't just the product of the gym alone.

They often talked about what "gear" they used and what it did for them, but I had done some research about it and the thought of sticking a syringe into my gluteus maximus made me feel sick, but just looking at the other guys and how their physiques bulged with muscle left me very frustrated.

No one was training harder than me; I was hitting the gym religiously four times a week. I never missed a session like some of my new mates who would go AWOL on a leg day. I knew that I had put off taking the gear for long enough and I think it was around June that I finally made up my mind that I needed to take gear to get anywhere near the size of the big guys at O'Malley's.

I had really no idea what to take, how to take it, and how long I would have to stay on it. My only source of information was my gym buddies who, no disrespect to them, had limited knowledge themselves.

I got told the best steroid to use would be deca duraboline and the reason behind using this was that it was very anabolic and the gains that I would get would be good quality lean ones. What they didn't tell me was that I should have used a testosterone base to counteract the aptly named "Deca Dick". This is a condition where one's libido is lowered to that of a sloth. I wasn't told this and unfortunately in later years had to find out the hard way, or should I say floppy way.

I purchased ten vials of deca and five syringes and needles and I was told that I would have to use each needle twice. Now even to my naive ears this didn't seem a good idea. I wasn't thinking about the obvious sterility implications though, I was more worried that the needle would be blunt after the first injection and the second one would hurt like hell. All I was told is "you stick the syringe into the top right of your arse".

I got the stuff home, waited until my Dad had gone out and filled the syringe with the oily contents. I looked at the green needle attached to it; it looked huge, just the thought of sticking this into my skin made me feel sick, but then I thought what the others looked like and after much hesitation, I dropped my baggies.

I didn't have a clue, didn't clean the area, I just put the needle to my upper "glutes" and pressed, while closing my eyes. It felt like someone shoving a knitting needle in to me. My hands were shaking and I could feel droplets of sweat forming on my forehead as I proceeded to push the contents into my body. I pulled the needle out quickly and a faint line of blood spurted out with it, the room went hazy and I woke up on the floor, shaking. Yes, okay, the first injection and I had fainted. I got to my feet and pulled my blood-stained baggies up and noticed the carpet had small traces of blood on it. I had to go to the kitchen and clean it up. My hands were still shaking as I scrubbed at the stain.

I sat down and thought: "No way am I doing this again, I don't care if I am not as muscular as the other guys." My arse felt wrecked and I felt as sick as one of football's proverbial parrots. I had to sit there for several minutes before I felt myself coming around.

The guys at the gym asked me how it had gone and they laughed when I told them that I wasn't going to do it again and what had happened. It brought about more merriment at my expense and Jay said that I was now an "addict of iron" and those "addicts" do anything they can in the pursuit of trying to get bigger. He told me that even he had felt daunted when he first began to inject himself and the others piped in with their stories about using gear for the first time. I listened to their stories and joined in the banter but no matter what they thought, the whole thing had felt wrong to me. I internalised that I wasn't an addict, no matter what Jay had said.

There was a new product called plant sterols and the hype suggested that it was as good as using steroids and that was music to my innocent ears. I will never forget drinking buckets of the green sickly sludge that promised everything, but delivered very little. I was trying everything that was on the market, most smelled and tasted like sweaty socks, but to me it was better than that pain in the arse: deca.

I was now no slouch in the gym; I trained naturally, hitting my body with all the basic exercises that shrieked both pain and growth. I was training with guys who were on the gear and although I couldn't lift as much as them, I ground out every last degree of movement from each set, until I was unable to push anymore and then I would use forced reps. This is where my training partner would give me an assist and I would push, pull or curl until I was completely dead. It was pain, recover and then more pain, but the mental image I had in my mind of being the guy with the massive muscles was all I needed. It was disheartening to realise that despite all my hard work, my gains were minimal.

I knew that at 12st 7lbs I had grown but I still didn't look like a bodybuilder. I felt disheartened, I wasn't fooling anybody, least of all myself. I knew that if I really wanted to have the X Man body, with the wide lats and massive quads, I would inevitably have to take gear but on the other hand, I didn't want the injections, somehow it felt all wrong. I had naively thought this was about being healthy and now it seemed like I would have to be some sort of junkie to progress. I was in a dilemma, I desperately wanted to look like the other guys, but apart from when I had a vest on, I didn't look like a bodybuilder.

It was even more evident when we went out for a night out. Women would hang around my mates because even in their civvies their bodies shrieked out to the crowds that they were built, but next to them I just looked like the "Average Joe".

I was getting fed up with training like hell and seeing only small gains and one afternoon while waiting for Jay to finish on the sunbed so I could take my turn, I was asking Chris – who was one of the regulars and who I sometimes trained with – what he thought the best oral steroid was. He told me about a drug called dianabol which he had used with other drugs, but I could use it on it own. He said that as a newbie, I would get some good gains off it, maybe even more that a stone in weight!

My ears pricked up when he said that. I was eager and enthusiastically badgered him for some more information. He agreed to get me some and went on to say that he would meet me outside the gym the next day about 12. I told him that I would get the money for him and we made our arrangements just as Jay's massive shadow loomed into view. He looked red and flustered. "Think I've sorted some gear out that's okay for me," I told him as he sat down. He sat down and chatted with us and then Bianca, the receptionist shouted to me: "You're on the sunbed next Jim!" "Going to leave it, let Jay have my remaining ones," I shouted back. I turned to him and said: "Don't know what you see in using sunbeds, they're bad for your skin and boring as fuck!" "If I get bored, I have a wank!" he replied in a nonchalant manner.

It took me several seconds to fully take in what he had just said. "Arrrrrrrrrr you dirty fucking bastard," I exclaimed as I realised that it was sometimes me who followed him onto the sunbed. The whole room was in hysterics by now and I just stood there shaking my head in mock disgust and thought that's why he always went on for the full 15 minutes and not just the seven.

The next day, I waited patiently outside the gym for Chris to arrive. It was obvious why I was lurking and I was hoping that Chris would be a bit more covert when he arrived, but subtlety wasn't in any of my new friends' vocabulary. I heard a loud toot that seemed to go on for an age, then a dramatic whoosh of air brakes, then Chris finally got out of this huge truck and came up to me with a beaming face as though the dramatic performance with his truck was an everyday event, which thinking about Chris's character it probably was.

Chris was one of the doormen from one of the town's main pubs and was loud in every area of his life. You didn't need a phone with Chris; you could hear him in the gym even when he was in reception. He was a good guy to train with but you got a lift home with him at your peril. He used to drive what seemed a few inches from the cars in front and road rage with him was definitely a chronic disease. He was forever in disputes with other drivers, mainly I suspect because he didn't know the Highway Code.

After all the attention he had brought to himself by screeching his truck to a dramatic stop, he then proceeded to hand me the dianabol as though he was sneaking it through customs at the airport. He looked up and down the street several times and then beckoned me closer and then slipped them to me as he kept watch.

The "dbol" came in a pink box and was from India. I sat down with Chris and he went through how I should take them. I would have to pyramid them which meant taking one a day for a week, then increase them every week until I was on six and then tapering them back down until you came off by using half a tablet. I knew some of the side-effects of taking steroids and when I was on my own, I nervously gulped down my first tablet. I was so naive that as soon as I swallowed it, I waited as though it was going to make my body explode or I would suddenly develop what bodybuilders call "bitch tits". I always liked having a big chest but one like Dolly Parton's that some guys get through taking gear was my worst nightmare.

The "gear" had a placebo effect on me straight away, although it would probably take over two weeks to fully get into my system. I felt stronger even after the first few days and I was feeling a lot more secure that the "Dolly Parton tits" would not make a guest appearance at any time soon.

I was more psyched up than usual and it seemed to help me focus even more when I was training. The poundage that I was able to train with was increasing and I was now on a par with some of the guys I knew at O'Malley's.

I was even able to use the maximum weight we had at the boxing club. We had two 20s and two 10s loaded on each dumbbell bar and then we could squeeze the collars on. Then we would play Russian roulette by doing flies with the precariously loaded bars. We would lie flat on a bench holding two dumbbells above your chest then lowering them down to the side, before tensing your chest and bringing the weights back up to the finishing position. The only problem we had was that they were loose discs held on flimsily by collars that were sadly worn and every now and again they would lose their grip and you would hear the weights thundering to the floor, closely followed by the other dumbbell and sometimes for the finale, me or one of the other guys overbalancing and plummeting to the floor.

I found that my appetite for both food and training was increasing. It wasn't by choice that I ate more; it was just that my body demanded it. I was hitting all the basics with even more gusto. I had stopped training with Jay by now because working out with him had become very hit and miss and now I just joined in with whoever was training the same body part as me. The scales were reading that I was over 13 and a half stone, a stone heavier than I had ever been. It didn't matter to me that much of it was water; all that I saw was that I looked bigger.

It was around this time that my brother Dave came down to visit me and my dad. He hadn't seen me for a few weeks and his first reaction to my metamorphosis was one of shock. I was closing in on 14 stone and now people could see that I was beginning to look more and more like a bodybuilder. I was happy to take my top off and do some posing in front of him. I could see that he was impressed and his reaction was one that I wanted. I didn't want to look like an ordinary guy anymore; I wanted to be recognised for what I was: a bodybuilder.

I was well into my second packet of dianabol and I was on six a day when I slowly began to notice that my throat felt sore. At first I thought that I had caught some kind of virus and I just carried on and used various over-the-counter medications for infections, but nothing seemed to help. It got to the point that I was having problems swallowing anything. Eating food or ingesting liquids became a major chore. I would take a throat lozenge and then try to digest food or a protein drink and then cringe in pain like I had swallowed a handful of razor blades.

I put up with it for a few more days until finally I had to go and see my doctor. I never gave it a thought that she would suspect anything, but I could see by her face that because she had known me for a number of years that her appraisal of my new-found appearance was making her slightly suspicious. After examining me and asking leading questions about my increased weight, she then interrogated me further and asked me that apart from the fact that I was spotty, had a face as round as the moon and I also had thrush, was I using anabolic steroids?

I don't think that she had to be Sherlock Holmes to guess that I was. I think as well as the physical indicators, my new style of dress, complete with baggies and oversized sweat shirt with the monogram "XXXL" gave her a slight clue. I eventually admitted that I had and she went on to lecture me about the serious health issues connected with their use. It seems that the orals that I had been taking had caused the thrush and now what was needed was a course of antibiotics.

After being appropriately chastised, I left the doctors feeling totally pissed off. It meant that I could no longer take the dianabol and worse than that, I would have to come off straight away and not taper the dosage. Cold turkey, it is called, and for a good reason. Psychologically, I was already feeling rough as hell and as the days went on, I felt like a junkie kicking his habit. I could feel my body already shrinking in anticipation but it seemed that anabolic steroids were just not meant for me.

I don't know if it was coming off the gear or just the feeling that I would never be as big as my peers, but I was depressed. I knew my natural genetics wouldn't give me the body I desired. I no longer wanted to add a bit of muscle, now I wanted to look huge, but it seemed as though there was no way forward. I felt like I was in a dark pit without any light filtering in and this was compounded further a few weeks later when I found out the funding for my job at the boxing club was coming to an end.

It came like a bolt out of the blue. It wasn't just the job; it was the great atmosphere the place had. I had made some good friendships with the other two instructors who were just as fanatical about the iron as I was. We had all spent many hours chatting about competing one day. Mike was about six feet tall and in clothes he looked like a slim bloke but if he wore a vest, you could see every muscle clearly defined. Rob, on the other hand, was "Mr Genetics" himself. We reckoned he got bigger just from looking at the weights. He was a true natural, his body responded to everything he did. It was tough training with him, not because the workout was hard but it felt infuriating to see him explode with muscle while he apparently just plodded through workouts and the inclination to drop a weight on him through sheer jealousy was definitely hard to fight at times.

I was back to training naturally again but something felt wrong, the massive overload of adrenaline that I always felt when pumping the iron had deserted me. For me the huge pump both mentally and physically that I had felt on the gear was what I was missing. The guys said that all I could hope for now was to retain some of the gains I had made and that really pissed me off. I had worked my arse off getting to nearly 14 stone and now I could see by the scales that my weight, no matter how hard I worked, was decreasing.

The days seemed long; I missed working at the boxing club and the daily banter. There was always something going on to make you laugh, now I sat at home when I wasn't training, scanning the papers for jobs.

I wasn't idle for long though. We were lucky in those days, there were plenty of vacancies. Don't ask me why I went for a driving job, the only thing I can think of if I remember correctly was that they gave me a van and I thought that would make travelling to the gym easier.

So my life as an operative with Telemeter Rentals began. It was the most bizarre job I've ever done. It required me to travel around Manchester, Oldham and Warrington, interviewing people who couldn't get credit normally and then decide if it was appropriate to install a television and video that had a meter secured on it and worked by putting in pound coins.

It was as dangerous as hell and as I told the guys at the gym, I never knew what each day would bring. Would I have to remove a television from a house full of skinheads? Would I be greeted by a pit bull terrier when making enquiries about what had happened to the television?

We had loads of people abscond with the sets, some faster than others. I came back a month later to one house in Salford to find it had metal shutters on it. A neighbour informed me that they had done a "moonlight flit" the same night that it had been installed.

I remember on one occasion I had to collect the rental money from a set in Stockport. It had been installed for a few months and all seemed to being going well, but on this occasion when I arrived, the lady, who must have weighed about 20 stone, opened the door with a small towel wrapped around her waist to protect her modesty. After a brief conversation, I started to empty the meter, only to find it had been broken into. The woman turned from being this gentle and softly spoken lady into this foul-mouthed harlot when I told her that I would have to remove the set because it was company policy to do so, when any signs of tampering had taken place. I had to pick both the television and video up together while trying to stop her from knocking them out of my hands, as I knew that if I only removed one at a time, she would have simply locked the door behind me and prevented me taking the remaining equipment.

I thought "just reach the door Jim, she'll stop when you get outside because she won't want the neighbours to see her semi-naked", but she kept coming, even when I got to the gate. The towel was now hanging loose and she began shouting at the top of her voice and was trying to pull me back, but I managed to get the van open. By now some of the neighbours had come out to see what the commotion was all about and some of them started joining in with the verbal abuse. I quickly locked the doors and scrambled into the driver's seat, but she started pounding on the driver's window with her fists and screaming at me.

"Get the car moving Jim, and she'll give in," I thought to myself and started to drive off slowly. She may have been overweight but she wasn't giving up without a fight and to my horror, she had now abandoned the towel completely and was running at the back of the van shouting obscenities at me. I could see her in all her glory in the driver's mirror, her whole body trembling and shaking with the effort of running. I don't know why but it was hypnotic for some strange reason, yet also surreal, but that sort of summed up my job at times; totally surreal!

My mates at the gym used to be in stitches about what I did for a living. My new job was definitely eventful and it was stressful too, you had to put yourself in situations where you would sooner not be, but it also made me more determined to get bigger. In my mind I thought that if I got as huge as some of my friends, then the situations I encountered would be easier to deal with. I knew I wanted to create a barrier between me and the world and my suit of armour would be the huge muscles that I would develop.

My fellow gym mates said I would just have to get used to injecting myself because for bodybuilders that was a way of life and even some of the so-called naturals used gear. I just couldn't face it though and carried on training naturally. My body weight went down to below 13 stones. It didn't matter to me that it was probably water weight that I had mostly lost, I internalised that I had the choice of being the smallest bodybuilder at the gym, getting thrush or fainting every time I had an injection, Hobson's Choice or what?

Although the guys used gear themselves, looking back, some didn't seem to have much idea what they were doing as none of them had ever competed and the sole aim for them was to scare the living shit out of any would-be troublemakers at the club.

I knew that I had to find someone who had the experience of being a successful bodybuilding competitor, because this is what I wanted to do. For me it wasn't just about getting huge, it was about being as my friends would say "ripped". I didn't want to just be a "bar body" either; this was where a person would only work the top half of the physique and not train the quads. I had seen a guy like that who used to come into the boxing club. He used to tell us about the top shows he had done in South Africa, his native country, and we were like blotting paper to his every word. The word around the gym was that he had a quality physique. It wasn't until one of the guys spotted him covertly sneaking into the changing rooms that his secret of wearing three pairs of tracksuit bottoms was found out.

Apparently he looked like he had two different bodies; the top half hard, defined and muscular and the legs like Twiglets. It wasn't unusual to see guys like this though; people often changed their minds while in the gym and put off training their legs. The reason was that it often involved having to do exercises like squats and stiff-leg dead-lifts which were both excruciating and exhausting.

Obtaining accurate information in those days couldn't be done by simply pressing enter on your computer. Word of mouth is how most people gathered information, so if the person advising you was wrong then you could end up inhibiting your progress or in the case of steroids, seriously affecting your health.

It was around this time I met a female bodybuilder who had competed in some top shows and was very well known. Paula trained with another female who had recently won the British Championship and my initial meeting with them was at the hack squat machine which is used to develop the quads. They both approached me in cut-down vests and shorts that highlighted their huge and defined legs and in a bass tone asked if they could join in with me. I had seen both these ladies use massive weights on the machine and meekly informed them that I had finished and it was "all theirs". I was used to feeling inferior to the other guys, but now I sat and watched in awe as they used the weight I had been struggling with and then proceeded to load the bar up with even more weight. I could hear the slow deflation of any ego that I might had previously been building with every rep they grunted out!

It was in the reception area later that I summoned up the courage to talk to them. Paula lived near me and I offered her a lift back home. We became good friends after that and she gave me loads of advice regarding training, diet and steroids.

I knew that I would need to use gear and that Paula was probably the most educated person I had met on the subject. It was through talking with her that I found injecting was less toxic on the liver than orals and that it was essential to follow good protocols of hygiene and that by having a simple bath, it made injecting easier because the skin became more compliant and easier to inject into. It was during one of our conversations at her home that she suggested using deca and sustanon for my first course and she went on to explain that as a male you needed to use a base course of testosterone and the sustanon would add more bulk.

I asked her if she could get me some and she went upstairs and came back with two multi vials in her hand. There were 10mls in each bottle and as I studied the labels, I felt the same uneasy sickly feelings I had when I had previous injected myself. I looked at her nervously. It was obvious she had used steroids, her muscles were not quite as big as some of the lads', but they were so much more defined, her voice was deep and she had faint facial hair on her face.

But what I noticed more was that she looked more like a bodybuilder than I did. It was this thought that made me more determined. I asked her if she would help me do the first few injections and she laughed and said: "You're not nervous are you?" She didn't need an answer, it was written all over my face. I could see she was amused but she was trying to keep her face straight and she said: "Okay, use the shower first and then I'll come up and sort you out!" I laughed as I stood up and said: "Cheers Paula."

I knew this was it. I wanted to be big and cut and this was what I had to do to achieve it. I would just have to get used to it, I said to myself, as I got undressed and watched as the hot water rippled down my body. I lathered the soap over my nether regions and then as I was drying myself, I heard Paula coming up the stairs. "Are you ready?" she enquired through the door. I thought "ready as I'll ever be". "Yep Paula, come in," I replied.

I could see that she had the two syringes and they were filled with the golden-coloured liquids. The needle glinted in the light of the bathroom as spray squirted into the air when she removed the air bubbles. I closed my eyes and grimaced, waiting for the sickening pain, but it never came. I heard her say "right you're done" and she got back up off her haunches. I couldn't help but smile, there had been very little pain and now I was going to at last be able to get the body I wanted. I turned to Paula and hugged her like I had just won the lottery, such was the relief, and she told me that she would help me with my next few injections.

We became good friends and began to hang out a lot together; I was now, under her supervision, able to inject myself without feeling faint. I was also training with her. She put most men to shame and she put me through session after session of hardcore, unforgiving workouts. I loved it. She knew how to train, it wasn't hit and miss like some of the guys, she was driven and I think that she recognised in me the same desire that she had. The guys filled their boots and subjected me to much mickey taking but I didn't care, she was training for the top competitions and I felt privileged to be able to train with her.

I liked her company. She was knowledgeable and funny, we began to spend a lot of time together. There was no romance, I thought at the time that we both fancied the same kind of people, mainly very feminine-looking women, but there was a moment though when the results of too much dry white wine nearly took their toll. We looked at each other and suddenly she became beautiful and her lips looked like they were dilating as they sucked me in. Suddenly we were kissing; her lips were wet and warm. I could feel myself becoming aroused; we began tearing at each other's clothes. The dimly lit room flickered with the light from the television as I started to embrace her and then I felt her rock hard arms that were like columns of steel, her legs that now entwined mine held me firmly like a vice. It was only when I got daring enough to touch her chest that I really freaked!

Instead of feeling soft, giving, supple breasts, I felt a chest that had no movement and was much more developed than my own. I could feel my ardour slowly dying, but I carried on kissing her, I didn't want to stop, but now I was slowly realising that I could feel faint stubble on her face. I am ashamed to say that I reacted like a virgin who someone was trying to defile and jumped up as if I had been electrocuted and quickly turned the light on.

I don't know if I did it to check if someone hadn't substituted Paula for a bloke or I was so scared that certain other parts of her anatomy might have been enhanced too and they would have put mine to shame. I felt embarrassed about the way I had acted and made an excuse, but I think Paula was relieved too. I don't know if she had an inkling of her true sexual preference when she was with me, but the last time I saw her, she was happily living with another lady as her partner.

Getting ripped

IT WAS late December 1995; I had got a new job with W.F. Demmy as a driver. The position was a very physical job and meant longer hours, a lot more driving but at least I didn't have to wear a gum shield and protective body armour when conversing with customers. I knew that my physique was improving but I was getting older and if I ever was going to compete, it would have to be soon.

It was in the January of 1996 that I first decided to compete. I knew I wanted to. I had learnt a lot from Paula about training, but I still had very little idea about how to diet, let alone how to compete. I looked through the pages of the bodybuilding magazines and saw there was a show at Mansfield. I hadn't a clue that this was a prestige competition; my sole aim was to compete just once.

I had a problem though: Paula, the only person I knew who would be able to help me, was working away, so I just set out a plan that I thought would be the best. I had read through some of Paula's old diet diaries when I had been at her house a few months before. All that I could remember from them was that they were low in fat and carbohydrates, but high in protein.

The following will absolutely prove that I either fell asleep or I developed amnesia when trying to recollect what Paula had written, but here is the diet that I devised, which was probably one of the worst in bodybuilding history. My plan was to have six egg whites and one yolk plus 30 grams of porridge oats, my dinner-time meal was tuna and white pasta, protein shake for after my workout and tuna and white pasta again for tea and that believe it or not was it.

I worked around 48 hours a week, went to the gym, did my cardio and I would go home and collapse. I went from being a very loving and chatty boyfriend to a catatonic mess. It got to such a point that my new girlfriend thought I was having an affair because I had no energy to make love and the only conversation she got from me was the odd grunt, before I fell asleep.

For 20 weeks I did this and I kept strictly to my plan. I went from 14 stone to 12 stone and when I showed Paula, who was home on a visit, she was amazed how ripped I was. I was ripped alright but I could barely stand up, I was so weak and I still had another seven days of work and training.

At work, conversations passed over me like I was in a fog, people's voices floated and occasionally rudely interrupted my thoughts, because I suddenly would become aware that they were talking to me and all I could think was "leave me alone" as I looked at the clock to see when my next feed was.

I remember being in the Transit van that I drove and I was handballing heavy bags out to my friend Paul. The next thing I knew I ended up hurling myself out of the van and stumbling into Paul and knocking him flying too, and when I looked back the bag was still there in the same spot, it hadn't move an inch.

Now every bodybuilder will tell you that three to four days out you start the process of increasing the amount of carbohydrates in your body to ensure that the muscles have more of a supply of glycogen and the muscles look full and hard. Now this is true, unless you get a stomach bug like me and have chronic sickness and diarrhoea. It happened four days out, I couldn't keep anything down and even simple training like a set of chins hurt.

I was so driven and wanting to do my first competition that nothing was going to get in the way. I didn't realise that most bodybuilders tapered down their intensity during the last couple of weeks and had the last three days, when they were carbohydrate storing or "carbing up" as it is usually called, completely off. But not me, I was training despite throwing up until finally nature stopped me in my tracks just three days before I was due to compete. It was unfortunate that I was wearing a pair of red baggies. I've heard of people following through before, but it had never happened to me. Then, sure enough during a set of rows, the inevitable happened; too much force, too weak a stomach and disaster struck!

In one of life's defining moments, there I was in the middle of the gym, no change of clothes and all I knew was that I had soiled my baggies and the stench was already filtering to my nostrils. I could feel the warmth and any moment now I was expecting seepage to appear from under my baggies. It was time for action. I had to get out of there, I don't think the guys had even seen me move so fast, and I dashed through the gym. Through reception, blanking everyone, but no doubt leaving a vapour trail in my wake.

I dived into my Transit van and pushed the pedal to the metal. It felt disgustingly warm as it trickled down my baggies and it felt like I was sat on a cow pat, but I wasn't going to stop and take a peek. When I arrived home, my girlfriend Linda thought I had hurt myself such was my distress as I rushed past her to the bathroom, but the odour soon reached her and her sympathy turned to both disgust and laughter as she followed me to the toilet.

So in the end my "carb up" was a sachet of dioralite which is used to rehydrate people when they are suffering from sickness and diarrhoea, and whatever else I could keep down without being sick.

Two days before the competition, Linda helped me shave all the hair off my body. I ensured that I did the more sensitive areas myself as the posing briefs I had bought left little to the imagination, so it was essential to get very close indeed.

Now came the fun part. On stage you have to be as dark as possible under the strong lights so we used Pro Tan. My girl helped me spray up, she told me she had some experience of doing similar work to this as she had previously creosoted her dad's fence at home. I couldn't believe how dark it was, even the first coat, it transformed me from a pasty white shaven ghost into a dark physique that highlighted every cut in my now ripped body.

The metamorphosis was now complete. I had turned from the caterpillar into the butterfly, and I now looked at last like a competitive bodybuilder, small but definitely ripped to shreds.

Linda, my best friend Mike and I got together the day before to go to Mansfield in the Transit van. It was bit risky using the van as it belonged to work and it wasn't supposed to be used for me to journey about at weekends. So I couldn't risk driving on the motorway, for fear of breaking down, so, we took the scenic route and ended up getting completely lost.

It wasn't the best idea that I had ever had to drive to a place I had never been to before while being so depleted. However, we finally got there and found out there was a local football match going on and a lot of the bed and breakfasts were fully booked up. After a lot of anxiety on my part we finally got one. Its exterior, though a little scruffy, far exceeded the interior. It was a mismatch of rooms and furniture. My girlfriend and I were shown a "double room" that just about fitted a double bed and I think Mike ended up in a room the size of a broom cupboard.

We went out to the local pub and got some quizzical looks about why I looked as though I had the colour of a black man and was so obviously white. I think they thought I was a Michael Jackson in reverse. I had a few glasses of wine to settle my nerves, and then we went back to the bed and breakfast for some "sleep". If you could call it sleep. I went through the night trying to, but I spent much of the night making endless trips to the toilet, so many in fact that I wore a trench in the carpet and every time I went, I would have a quick sneak preview in the mirror. Such is the paranoia of a bodybuilder especially the night before. My reflection at various stages looked fat, skinny and waterlogged.

I must have slept about two hours all night. We got up at six for a final spray of the tan, then my girlfriend and Mike went down for breakfast and I had a coffee. I was so nervous I couldn't eat anything.

Even the walk up to the venue which was only a few hundred yards away seemed to take forever and I could feel any confidence that I had waning as I watched the huge people queuing outside. They all seemed to be gathered in little cliques and they all looked like bodybuilders should look. I nearly turned away at this point and but for Mike and my girlfriend, I probably would have. But inside I went and nervously approached the sign-in desk to give my posing music and get my numbers. I had decided to compete in two categories; the over-35s and the first-timers in the hope I may get a trophy.

The venue filled up and I couldn't believe the amount of people coming to watch. I sat there in the audience and watched the MC's mouth moving, I know he was saying something, but I was in another place and time until my girlfriend nudged me and asked if I was okay? I nodded my head. I had been thinking back to the time that I got my first weight kit and how I had looked at the pictures of the physique stars and never dreamt that one day I would actually compete in a show.

The hall was at near capacity and as I looked back I could see that there were very few seats left. I could hear the laughter and banter and rustling of food packets being opened as I sat there in my war paint of Pro Tan. I could feel my nerves tingling the longer I sat there and I just wanted to get it over with. I kept thinking that maybe I wasn't good enough to be there? Maybe I would get laughed at? Maybe I could just slink off home and pretend today had never happened?

They call it flight or fight and believe me at times it was a toss-up to which I would do, but something inside me demanded that I take my chances on stage so I just sat there, alone in my self-made pool of emotions. I looked at the clock. We seemed to have been there for ages and then in a blink of an eye, the MC came on stage and announced that all over-35s should now go backstage. I was relieved that Mike was allowed back with me. I felt slightly anxious and there was a hive of activity, you could feel the nervous energy emanating from guys as they started their preparation.

You could hear gasps of breath as people started using the weights to pump themselves up with. There were another 16 competitors and one guy looked about 20 stone. He stood in the corner doing single arm dumbbell curls, his arms looked like one of my quads. I could feel the self-belief in my own abilities sinking lower and lower. It felt intimidating being here and I was going to be judged against guys who probably had a lot more experience than me, but as I looked around me and met some of the stares of the other guys, I closed my eyes and gritted my teeth and grabbed a pair of dumbbells that were free and started to do some bicep curls and shoulder work.

I still had my t-shirt and baggies on as one by one the other competitors started to strip off and they all looked good. I was already psyched out, I had done all the wrong things, I shouldn't have looked at anyone else, the words that Paula had told me came flooding back: "Concentrate on yourself and keep calm." I was lost in my thoughts as I felt Mike put some oil on my back. "You're looking great pal," he whispered to me as I was called into the line of competitors waiting to go on stage. The MC called us on and the crowd loudly cheered and shouted out their favourites' names. I stood there posing my lats, chest, tensing my arms and quads and to my amazement I was called out first and as I went a few of the crowd screamed "ripped to fuck". This is one of the best accolades you can get from a bodybuilding crowd.

I started to feel confidence pulsing through my veins as I pushed out yet another pose. The hall was filled with the chaotic noise of people screaming on the competitors and I slowly started to realise the guy they were shouting "ripped" at was number three. I don't know if it was nerves or I just had lost all sense of who I was, but I had to stop and take a long lingering look at my tan-stained number before I realised they were shouting for me! I felt the tension leaving my body and then my face creased not into a forced grin, but with a smile as wide as the Grand Canyon. I felt alive as I finished off the latest round with an all-out, balls to the wall "most muscular" pose that made my body shake with the energy I put into it.

I went on to get multiple call-outs and my new "fan club" were with me all the way. I had felt alone when I first set foot on the vastness of the stage, but now I felt at home. The final round was between me and the big guy of about 20 stone and one of the local gym owners who was vastly experienced. They certainly got their money's worth, moving us from various sides into different poses. I came off the stage thinking I had got third place and I was well pleased, but the results wouldn't be in until after the evening show.

I came to the front of the stage into the main forum to be greeted by my girlfriend and Mike; it was crazy the transition that had happened to me from the nervous individual who had gone backstage to the hyper, smiling and confident guy that now was busily chatting away to everyone. I had quite a few seasoned bodybuilders asking me how I got so ripped and some saying they thought I had won it.

I sat back to watch the other classes, but I couldn't concentrate and they seemed to pass in a haze until Mike announced: "They're asking for the first-timers to go backstage Jim!" I wasn't hesitant now, I was looking forward to being back on stage and I just gave Linda a kiss and followed Mike to the rear of the stage. Some of the guys nodded to me as I dumped my bag and started to get undressed. I wasn't scared of showing my physique now and this time I remembered to concentrate on what I was doing as I started to pump my biceps with greater and greater intensity.

I was on a high, full of adrenaline, and I could sense the anxiety from my opponents as Mike told me they were taking nervous glimpses at me. Time seemed to be going faster now; I was in mid-flow of doing some dumbbell pullovers to work my chest and lats when we were called on stage. Mike rubbed some more oil on my back as I took my place in line with the six other competitors.

The guy at the back curtain ushered us on to massive roars from the crowd. I set my body, pushing hard on each muscle so that they would stand out and then did the "smile" as Paula had told me to do. Like the over-35s class I got the first call-out, the guy to my right looked massive and cut as well and the other bodybuilder, number five to my left was the local favourite. His name was met with a crescendo of noise.

Every time a mandatory pose was announced the crescendo of noise for number five reverberated around the room, but it didn't affect me as I hit each and every pose as though my life depended on it. After the last comparison, we returned to the line-up. I waited as the next call-out came but my name wasn't mentioned. I waited in vain as every round passed me by and slowly I could feel my self-confidence ebbing again and the smile slowly disappearing. That was it, I got the first and only call-out and as the MC shouted: "The judges are happy, you'll see these guys tonight!" I trailed off the stage last, my mind filled with the thought that I had been simply outclassed by the other guys.

In both the free posing rounds, I did exactly the same poses to the same music; such was my limitation in the art of posing and my music choice. The posing went something like this, quarter turns, displaying chest, back, biceps, legs and abs and the finale was "traps over" which is a pose that should display a complete muscular physique. The art of posing should be the ability to move from one pose to another gracefully. Mine was more akin to the most wooden of actors; no fluidity, no originality and definitely no style.

The interval arrived and my brother turned up, with my two nephews and our friend Barry. I had been told that in the evening show there was no judging and we could eat. So, unfortunately I had vacated the building when everyone arrived. I was in the van, munching on a death by chocolate cake; no careful slicing, just breaking the cake in half and trying to stuff as much down my gob as possible. After 20 weeks of dieting, the only thing I could think about was my cake. It wasn't until the doors of the van were opened to an audience of my brother, girlfriend, nephews and my friends that I realised I looked somewhat strange; a man covered in chocolate tan with additional chocolate cake plastered across his face.

It was a lengthy interval waiting for the evening show to start but eventually, the over-35s were called backstage, and this time I was much more relaxed as I knew the results were already in and this was merely a demonstration for the crowd. We went through the various call-outs and then the competition MC shouted "pose down". This was the cue for everyone to rush forward and to do random poses against each other. Lots of pushing, scrambling in order to get the prime spot on stage, all the crowd were shouting out their favourites' names and then suddenly the music stopped and we were asked to line up at the back of the stage.

My mouth felt so dry with nerves. All the preparation I had done, the dieting, cardio and it all came down to this. Medals would be given out to the guys who hadn't finished in the first three. I closed my eyes and listened to the announcer, desperately hoping I wouldn't hear my name and then it was suddenly over and he was asking for the first three to step forward and my name was among them.

I couldn't believe it. Soiling the baggies and increasing production of Japan's export of tuna to the UK over the last 20 weeks had all been worth it. Now the big guy of over 20 stone stood next to me and on the other side stood the experienced, well known competitor. When the MC announced third place I was ready to take the applause, but they called out the big guy. It was like a dream, I was in shock when he announced the winner as Jim Moore and the crowd were applauding and shouting my name.

All the times when I had wanted to give up, the times when it had reduced me to tears, times when I had doubted I could complete this journey, had all just been forgotten in the euphoria of this moment. I posed for the camera with my winner's bronze statue, and then I went backstage to see my family and friends. It all felt surreal, I kept looking at the beautiful bronze statue that depicted a bodybuilder in an Atlas-type pose. I kept thinking I would wake up and find it was just one of the dreams I had been having recently.

I was shaking with excitement as I drifted back to my seat with Linda draped over my arm. I tried to sit down and act kind of nonchalantly as if this wasn't a big deal to me, but inside I was racing. A couple of people at the back of me leant over and congratulated me. It was like being some kind of celebrity and time once again evaporated and I was on cloud nine until Mike reminded me that I had to go back on stage for the first-timers' competition. I realised that a full hour and 20 minutes had gone by.

The atmosphere had changed when I stepped on stage again; the crowd was subdued and as we did our pose down, it was obvious one of the guys had many followers in the audience and they seemed angry. The medals were given out to the to the guys who had finished outside the first three and seeing as I had only had one call-out in the morning judging, I presumed my name would be among them, but it wasn't. I was left on stage with the guy with the big quads and number five.

It became evident as we were taken through the mandatory poses that the huge volume of noise emitting from the crowd that was crushing out any other shouts wasn't for me or the guy with the massive quads. As the crowd quietened, straining to hear the MC, muffled cries of disappointment slowly rang out as the local lad was announced third; the guy with the big quads second and to a volume of hated calls of "he's no beginner" I was placed first. It seemed that the defeat of the local lad hadn't gone down well, but much to his credit he walked across the stage and shook my hand. It was my first show, I had won two first trophies, I was both elated but upset that I had been called a cheat.

I came off stage thinking: "Fuck you, I've half killed myself for this and now they are trying to make me feel shit because I beat their guy." A group of people came out of the now more sedate crowd. I could see them approaching me and I thought "here we go, I'm going to be lynched" so I clenched my fists and thought that if it was going to go off, I was not going to just stand there and take it, but to my relief because I was shattered both mentally and physically they were full of praise and congratulation, they told me not to mind the chants as they knew it was my first time on stage. I was totally overawed and thanked them for their kindness.

For me the day had been a rollercoaster of emotions and all I wanted to do was be with my friends and family. I got to where Linda and everyone was and they were in a party mood, but for me the "cheat" calls had taken the edge off what should have been a fantastic moment for me, and as I left the venue, I was thinking: "I've done what I set out to do and I never want to take my body through that again!"

That was the plan at the time and I was quite happy as we walked through the glass doors of the leisure centre into the warm summer night's air. Unfortunately I wasn't there when they made numerous calls for "Jim Moore" to come backstage; in both my naivety and excitement I had forgotten that there was an overall trophy for the best bodybuilder in the show and it wasn't until a few months later when I met one of the judges that I was told that I had been selected as the "overall" winner, but in my absence they had given it to another guy.

But never mind, I now had another challenge in front of me; the tradition of the after-show indulgence of how much crappy food you can eat. From my hazy recollection it started with three Big Macs, then more cake, chocolate and then retiring to my home, well no, not exactly, I should have said the kitchen. Much to the disgust of Linda, I now proceeded to open cupboard after cupboard in the eating frenzy from hell. I even ate the breakfast cereal. I did have some decorum and control though. I held back from eating the cat's food that had developed a certain allure to it at that moment in time. With my stomach now resembling an orange spacehopper, I bounced up the stairs to a hero's greeting by my girlfriend. "Hail the conquering hero" she expressed among a crescendo of snores.

Over the next few days I indulged myself in the finer foods of life; I would go into supermarkets and walk down aisles thinking "I see therefore I eat". I became our local baker's favourite customer; in fact I spent so much time in there, that they billed me for council tax.

The bloating, crippling stomachache that accompanied my feasting felt terrible, but the allure of being able to eat any goodies I liked prevailed but after about ten uncomfortable days and being two stone heavier, I'd had enough and went back to eating sensibly. I was back at work but found myself looking at the competitions, located at the back on the bodybuilding monthlies. I hadn't expected any of the successes that had come my way and now in my dreams and sometimes waking moments I replayed the scenes over and over again. I slowly became aware that my original plan that I had broadcast to anyone in earshot that I would compete once and only once was bullshit!

Taking it to the Brits

THE EUPHORIA of winning had been such a rush to my system. It was like heroin to an addict and my serotonin and dopamine levels were sky-high. I needed that "high" again and I rationalised that the only way that I could possibly get it again was to compete once more.

Unfortunately something seemed wrong. I was training, but after the high of winning came a low, like a heavy cloud that was threatening to squash me. The days seemed dark and cold; training became more like a burden. It was the anti-climax of competing that had left me feeling depressed, the dark winter nights were setting in and in my mind, the only warmth or happiness I could feel was thinking back to the days of being on stage.

The spark of light that erupted and brought life and intensity back into my life came as I perused the latest bodybuilding magazine. It advertised a show for the following year; it was the NABBA North qualifier for the British Championships and it was being held in Doncaster in April. I made up my mind to compete in it and I could feel the darkness floating away from my shoulders. As the days and weeks went on, I could feel my appetite for training come back, I was full of zest and vigour and the iron was my friend again.

I dieted through Christmas and New Year, my loved ones' wishes coming second to my tunnel vision of selfishness. Paula was now back home. I think she was stunned by what I had achieved and she had set out a diet plan for me to use in my next show. I did set out with the good intentions of following it to the word, but I became paranoid that the amounts that she set out for me to eat were too much. I am ashamed to say that I didn't take her advice and if she is ever reading this, sorry Paula!

In the end I just stuck to the same regime I had previously. I did use some of her ideas on pharmacology and I introduced a new drug called clenbuterol, which was used to treat asthma, but it had an excellent side-effect for bodybuilders. It acted as a thermogenic, which meant quite simply that you burnt up fat a lot quicker than normal. The negatives of the drug were that you shook like crazy, you felt hot as hell all the time, so you were either constantly sweating like you were in your own personal sauna or shaking like an alcoholic with delirium tremors. But this didn't bother us. All we saw was that it helped us lose the surplus body fat.

I still didn't like injecting myself but it was fast becoming part of my life along with the sweatshirts, belts, wraps and baggies which were loose-fitting tracksuit bottoms. I could now "pin" myself without flinching, well no that's a lie, I flinched quite a lot but now I could inject without fainting so things were definitely improving.

Each day I would wake up, down the same boring porridge and egg whites, stagger to the Transit van and go to do my cardio before work. I was so low on body fat that the only thing that hurt now when I was on the dreaded stationary bike was my arse. I had stopped the cross-trainer and treadmills because my cognitive ability to actually stay upright had long since gone.

I was a liability, not just in the gym but my job was suffering too. I would find myself just driving right past the places I had to drop off at and my colleagues thought I was crazy. I think Paul, who used to drive with me to help out with the heavier drops, definitely questioned my sanity after I went around a roundabout the wrong way, to much beeping of horns, gesturing, inappropriate finger movements and general fist-shaking. I think for him that was the final straw. After so many near-misses, he'd had enough of my driving. I was glad when he volunteered to take the wheel so I could munch on my second meal of tuna. Again the aroma wasn't Paul's favourite and he said something about the van smelling like a pair of nun's knickers!

I think in the end my fellow workers sent me to Coventry, but I never really noticed until after the shows when people would tell me about my indiscretions. At the time, I was more than happy that people were quiet around me and I didn't have to waste energy making conversation with non- bodybuilders about things that I regarded as trivial, but in retrospect I now realise that then I felt that anything not related to bodybuilding was to my mind "trivial"!

I think the time spent getting into condition is probably as near as a "straight doer" like me comes to being in prison. Granted there were no bars, only those in my mind. I couldn't sleep; I was so hungry that I would wake up from nightmares where I was raiding the fridge. You live your life not one day at a time, but from meal to meal and the sentence you serve is the time taken to get in condition. Your release date is the day of the show!

I was fast becoming a stalker too. I found myself following people down the road as they ate their takeaway and I would be behind them sniffing the beautiful aromatic smell that came from their food. Lucky for me they never saw me. I don't know what I would have said to this poor woman as I trailed behind her breathing in the elixir of the local chippy. "Excuse me missus can I smell your fish and chips?" And I don't think the magistrate would have believed that I was only stalking the ladies for their fishy aroma either.

Occasionally for a change I used to train at another gym called Newbodies, which was run by Dave who had been a top competitor. I came into the gym one night after working when I was so jaded I could hardly keep awake and Dave, seeing this and knowing I had a competition coming up, said to me to try this pre-workout drink called Ultimate Orange.

I thought why not and paid him for a couple of sachets. He mixed one for me and said it took about ten minutes to kick in. "How will I know?" I inanely replied. Well anyone who ever tried the old Ultimate Orange would know that was probably the dumbest question in bodybuilding history! It hit me like thunder; I was out of my seat and under the squat bar, lifting heavier and more reps than I had ever lifted before. Charging from squats to leg press and then hacks, heaving them with a frenzied, inhuman force, I just couldn't stop. My heart was beating through my chest and when I stopped training, I couldn't stop talking to anyone who would listen.

I then climbed into the van and was driving even crazier than when I was depleted. When I got home I couldn't rest; I cleaned the kitchen, living room and bedrooms and when my girlfriend came home at 8pm she found me mowing the lawn. She stood there, looking in amazement. I hated doing anything in the garden and mowing the grass in the dark was maybe giving her a clue that I wasn't quite myself. It was two o'clock in the morning before I began to calm down. I never bothered with it again. It was the best but also one of the worst feelings of my life.

The day of the show finally arrived and we packed the car to depart at six in the morning. The show didn't start until 12 and Doncaster was only about 50 miles away, but to the paranoid, depleted bodybuilder, nothing is left to chance. Arriving there at eight o'clock in the morning with Linda and my brother in tow, we decided to take in the town of Doncaster and get a refreshing cup of coffee. I don't think the gentlemen of the road who were sat together drinking their fine white cider could quite believe their eyes. At eight in the morning, in full regalia of baggies, sweats and glowing bright orange I strutted past them. They looked at each other as if to confirm what they were seeing was real, looked down at their beverages and back at me. I often wonder to this day if they believed they were having delusional episodes or maybe I was the catalyst to their cure.

We got to the venue and I went backstage and found out to my horror that there weren't any weights there for me to pump up with. In a panic, Linda said that she would find a sports shop and see if there was any equipment that she could buy. The call came for all novices to go backstage and as I arose, this giant of a guy stood up as well. He looked huge in his sweats, but unlike the other 20-stone guy I had defeated in my first show, this guy's face looked gaunt, the tell-tale sign of someone in good condition. Surely he had misheard, but no, he walked behind me, his shadow enveloping me. If he was trying to psych me out as bodybuilders do to each other before competitions, he was doing a great job.

At this moment, my girlfriend arrived backstage breathlessly, carrying a set of dumbbells. I looked at them and they were the brightest set of yellow weights I had ever seen. As I scrutinised them further, I could see that although they looked a decent size, they were plastic and weighed only 2lbs each.

It is true that we don't need massive weights to pump up with, but I think a budgie may have had more use for them than I could. She was standing there with beads of sweat on her forehead, and no doubt she had made a major effort to get them, so I picked them up and said they were perfect and kissed her.

We never did use the budgie weights though. My brother and I started to pump up using isometric exercises, and we used towels as resistance. It was at this stage that we were doing some side lateral raises, my brother pushing against my arms as I tried to raise them. I had my back to the big guy and by now I was convinced that my brother was right and he wouldn't look so good when he had taken his clothes off.

I was in the zone, concentrating hard when I saw my brother's face look in awe. He had seen the guy disrobe. I could tell by his expression that he wasn't just huge; he was cut to ribbons as well. I deliberately made no eye contact with him or any of the other competitors and I just tried to focus on what I had to do. I continued doing press-ups, slowly watching my blood-absorbed muscles maxing out.

I could hear one of the backstage helpers calling for the novices to get in line and after a hug from my brother I joined the line.

It was then I took stock of the other competitors. There were six of us, of very similar build. I felt confident that I was definitely on a par with them and then the light suddenly went as this monster physique took his place in front of me.

As we were introduced by the MC, we slowly walked on stage and I don't think many people saw me until we were directly in front of them. I was stood next to him; he was that big, I could feel his presence and the shadow he cast looked huge. I stood nervously flexing everything I had. I had been told never to look at my opponents until the trophies are handed out but I couldn't help it, I found myself transfixed and thought why the fuck is he doing the novices, he would win his weight class, he was that good, but most of all I thought why the fuck does he have to stand next to me?

The judges studied the line-up and then made the first call-out. No surprises, the huge guy I now knew as Colin due to the many people shouting out his name was called out first, then me and much to my angst they positioned me right next to "Mr Goliath" again. As the third guy joined the line-up, all I could think was "thank God for that, he looks similarly built to me".

We were taken through the poses and I was hitting them with everything I had, really pushing my quads through the floor as the judges called out "double bicep". I could hear my friends shouting out my name and this enthused me. I wasn't holding back, sweat was pouring off me and then I was suddenly pitched once more into the dark again. The MC had called for "side chest, any side" so I had turned and I now faced Colin, well I say faced, what I really mean was I now was directly looking at his chest. We struck the pose simultaneously. Colin's chest was so huge and he was that tall his chest acted as an umbrella for me, but my staunchest fan, my brother chose this opportune moment to scream: "You've got him Jim!" All I could think was that I wanted to get away from under his chest because nothing grows in the shade.

Towards the end even my brother had stopped shouting. It was a formality that Colin had won, the guy who was similar to me was given second place, but I was third. I had done it, I had qualified for the NABBA British champs and I couldn't have been happier.

I turned to shake hands with my opponents. My hand disappeared in Colin's bucket-like grip and any euphoria that I was feeling was dashed. All I could think as I surveyed "Mr Goliath" was "how the fuck do I beat you?"

The finals were in November in Dudley so there was time to improve but my driving seemed to be as bad as ever. The low carbohydrate diet I was on was causing havoc with my ability to recognise the parameters of the Transit, which resulted in a few prangs and the boss questioning my eyesight, but the truth was that the job had become second to my ambition to compete.

It was a rough time emotionally. After four years, Linda and I decided to split. It had been on the cards for a few months. She was an incredibly practical person and if you needed to arrange anything, Linda was your lady, whereas I was more emotional and lived life for the moment. Looking back I was selfish too. My life had changed that much since I had started competing that I had neglected to fully realise Linda's needs. I understand now in retrospect how bodybuilding can take over your life until you marginalise everything else that comes in the way of it, but at the time, I couldn't comprehend why Linda didn't want me to pursue my sport anymore.

We had drifted apart over the last few months to the extent that she came in from her running, me from my bodybuilding and our worlds or friends never met. We were together but isolated, and there was care on both sides but sadly no love. We had both been in denial, not wanting to hurt one another and avoiding the subject. I think it was a relief for both of us when I finally suggested that maybe we would be better off apart. We had become more like brother and sister over the last few months but it was still sad when we both recognised this and the morning when I helped her with her suitcase, I felt pangs of emotion as I watched her red car slowly disappear down the road.

I must have stayed there for several minutes, I knew that we were going to see one another and be supportive friends, but as I went back into the silence of the lonely room, I knew that I was going to really miss her company even if it had only been the odd grunt or acknowledgement of each other's existence.

Deep down inside I knew it was for the best. Linda would be able to pursue her goals and I would be able to submerge myself in my "hobby", well that's what I called it at the time, but I guess every kind of addict deceives himself or as the Simon and Garfunkel lyrics say: "A man hears what he wants to and disregards the rest."

Don't get me wrong, for me bodybuilding is a beautiful sport or lifestyle but it has to be kept in control because I know from my own experience and from the numerous other guys and girls I have helped over the years that if it isn't kept in check, it ends up taking over your whole life. At this time in my life though, I talked bodybuilding 24/7, I read bodybuilding and I ate and drank bodybuilding and now it seemed only right after Linda left that I tried to get a job where I could "work" bodybuilding.

One of the places where I used to deliver was a bodybuilding company in Sale and one day when I had dropped some packaging off, I was moaning about the work interfering with my bodybuilding, when I was offered the opportunity to work for them. For me at the time, it was a no-brainer and after serving notice at Demmy's, I left for a job that paid less, had few opportunities, fewer benefits, but enabled me to be able to train more. I think my old boss was happy to see the back of me. Well, if he wasn't, the heavily-dented Transit van was.

Working in the shop put me in touch with many of the top guys in the sport, although this was a double-edged sword as now I was told that the amount of gear I was using was what most of the female bodybuilders were on. Stan and Mick were regular customers, both had won the UKBFF Championships which for many people are the top amateur shows in the UK, but it was Ben, who had recently won the UKBFF Masters title, who I got to know well. His profession was jack of all trades; he was a real character and sold watches from the back of his car but he was also the guy who helped educate me about diet and what gear I should be on.

I listened to my new friends and began to take their advice and it was around this time that many underground steroid laboratories were coming to the fore, which meant that the drugs could possibly be made in conditions that were not very sterile. Some were fake, some under-dosed, and some as we all found out were nothing but some kind of oil. I remember that at one stage there seemed to be more fake steroids on the market than ever and one particular disgruntled mate of mine made the comment that he must have injected so much snide gear only containing oil that his joints must have been the most lubricated on the planet.

It became a lottery. You paid your money and took your chance; word of mouth was the main thing and customers would openly talk about what had given them good gains. It was through such a source that I started using a drug called liquid dianabol. Its reputation at the time was that it put on some "serious muscle tissue". Once those words are spoken, the iron brethren would take heed and follow. I often wondered whether if they said that digesting camel dung would add muscle, we would have eaten it.

Like the other guys I began using it but they didn't tell me the full side-effects, which I found out when I turned up for work after a couple weeks. The side-effect of frequent raging erections was quite distinct, especially as I wore baggies most of the time. One day the full scale of this hit and I had to spend the whole afternoon hidden behind the shop counter. I had to ditch my normal friendly customer care skills and on one occasion when a young lady who I knew and liked came into the shop, I had to direct her to products from the sanctuary of the counter, shouting at the top of my voice: "Left near your foot." I could see her thinking: "Why doesn't he just come from behind there and show me?" I smiled to myself that the product wouldn't be the only thing that I would be showing her if I stepped out to where she could see me.

You couldn't help but notice Ben. His car was covered in advertising by the people who sponsored him and he used this to adopt his Arthur Daley image of stopping in the street and selling complete strangers watches, supplements or whatever you needed.

Some people really disliked him, probably because they had bought something off him that didn't work, but to me he became good company. He would often call in the shop and spend time just chatting about bodybuilding. In fact it was quite common on an afternoon to see the guys congregate and discuss important issues such as what "shit", aka steroids, was good and what to avoid.

Being in the shop definitely had its merits. Sol the owner used to let me buy supplements at trade prices, but it also brought me into contact with people who were hugely respected because of their reputations for dealing with issues in very extreme ways. To protect these people from criminal proceedings and because I like my kneecaps where they are, I will refer to them, but not reveal any names.

My advice on various subjects was always being sought by customers and on one such occasion, a guy I knew came in, looking very irate and told me that he thought he had bought some "fake gear". He requested that I have a look at it. It didn't look right, the labels weren't on straight and I had never heard of the brand. So in an innocent and off-the-cuff remark, I agreed with the guy and said it may be fake as he had been on it for four weeks and seen no improvement. He thanked me for looking and went on his way. I never thought anything about it until I received a phone call from Mr X. His tone wasn't angry, just very matter-of-fact. He told me that as I worked in a shop, did I realise I was a sitting duck as anyone who had a problem with me knew exactly where I was?

I nervously told him that I would never disrespect him and asked him what the problem was. He told me that the guy had gone back to his supplier and told him that Jim Moore definitely knows this is fake and he wanted his money back. I couldn't believe this, all I did was offer some friendly advice and now I had upset one of Manchester's faces.

All I could think was: "Where is my passport, I need to emigrate right NOW!" I explained to him exactly what had gone on and apologised. There was a silence on the other end of the phone which seemed to last hours, but it was probably a few seconds. He told me that he accepted my apology and he hoped he wouldn't have to remind me again. The phone was abruptly put down by him, closely followed by a deep intake of breath by me. To say I was relieved was an understatement, I don't think my underwear was ever usable again!

There were many such occasions that I met guys like this. Sports like boxing and bodybuilding seemed to attract them. They didn't threaten, didn't swear, and didn't get angry. They didn't have to as their reputations preceded them. You learnt to treat them with respect, talk about bodybuilding and watch your words and have selective vision to what was going on around you.

I was really excited when Sol, the owner of the supplement company, asked me to accompany him to Wembley Arena to watch the finals of the UKBFF Championships. He had managed to get a stall selling his supplements and this was a great advertising opportunity for him to promote his company.

We drove down after work on a Friday night; he had booked rooms at the Hilton Hotel which was a stone's throw away from the venue. I was knackered when I arrived there and the bar was swimming with the who's who of bodybuilding. It was here I met one of the coolest guys I have known in bodybuilding. He was a black guy called Pat and he had previously been the middleweight champion, taken some time out and this was his comeback year. Sol bought me a drink and I got chatting to this blonde girl who was competing in the physique competition and was up against her sister. She was really dedicated and she had uprooted from Cornwall to come to Manchester to be trained by Kerry Kayes, who was a top coach and owner of a major supplements company.

I think it was Sol who introduced me to Pat and his mate. I learned more in the alcoholic hours that followed than any other time. He was full of information and I was like a piece of blotting paper to his erudite words.

He talked about the next day's competition and the people competing; the tactics, the gear and how he had gone to each qualifier to watch. He was wearing a woollen crew top and a pair of black trousers and to be honest, he looked like the average guy you see in the street. It wasn't until Sol said to him "let Jim see how you're built" that we staggered off to the toilets and he found a mirror and striped off to his waist. It was an amazing transformation; he had a top quality physique, with very few weaknesses.

The maturity and depth of his muscles were what I lacked and it was at this point that he asked how my physique was looking so drunkenly I stripped off too and we began to pose off against each other in the mirror. I don't know what the poor chap that came in as we were both hitting the most muscular pose thought, but he definitely presented as extremely nervous and he gave us both a quizzical stare before quickly disappearing into one of the cubicles and locking it behind him. Maybe having to squeeze past two semi-naked drunken muscular men wasn't a sight he was used to at the Hilton Hotel but the look he gave us was like one of the village virgins, awaiting the marauding Vikings.

We came out of the toilets after that and carried on drinking and talking until there was nobody left in the bar except staff. It was around 2am that I slurred my excuses and said that I needed to go to bed as I had to help set up the stall early in the morning. I couldn't believe it when Pat said he needed some sleep too as he was competing! I was totally stunned. I had forgotten in my drunken haze that he was competing early the next day, but he was the epitome of cool as he got up and shook my hand and thanked me for my company.

All I could think was that if it was me who was competing tomorrow, I would have been in bed early and I wouldn't have dared drink half as much as Pat. Most bodybuilders would have been watching what they eat, they may have had a drink but nowhere near as much as he had drunk. I don't know whose tab we put the drinks on but I bet it was expensive. We had drunk three bottles of wine before we staggered off to our rooms.

I woke up feeling dog rough; I hardly touched the breakfast and sat quietly while Sol tucked into a full English. My mind wandered to Pat and the amount of drink the three of us had put away. I couldn't help feeling that somehow he had jeopardised his chances because if he felt anything like I did, then all he would want to do is sleep.

I climbed in the van with Sol to go and set up our stall in the Wembley Arena. Later that day I spotted Pat on stage looking fantastic. He looked confident, sprightly and refreshed like he had a good night's sleep. All I could think was that I didn't know what he took to have that much energy, but I wanted him to hook me up with some because I looked the total opposite, dead on my feet and totally knackered!

The day was a long one. The arena was filled to capacity and buzzing with excitement and as the evening show began, you could sense the nervous energy as the competitors took to the stage to fight for the coveted title of British champion.

I got the chance to watch Pat; it was around eight o'clock in the evening before the class of around 20 of the top middleweights in the country took the stage. I was slumped in a seat snacking on a protein bar trying desperately to stay awake as he took second place against one of the best line-ups in the history of the UKBFF.

When I look back now I realise that maybe Pat's laid-back approach may have been beneficial to me too, but it's strange, although I always talked about going out the night before and relaxing, I never actually did it. I was always far too paranoid and thought that it would mess my chances up, so I always kept to my usual half naps and myriad of trips to the toilet, although later as you will read, I did refine my approach by introducing quite a revolutionary alternative to using the loo every five minutes. I purchased what became a quintessential bit of equipment for any competitive bodybuilder; it was called the "piss bucket"!

Ben offered to help me get ready for the NABBA Novice British Championship after I came back from the UKBBF finals. He designed a diet that looked at maintaining blood sugar levels by not just eating three or four meals but at least six. He divided the day into sectors, so that my body had adequate carbohydrates, proteins and fats. I began to feel less tired and as the competition neared, he manipulated my carbohydrates and added cardio. My body was beginning to look cut but this time I was keeping more of the muscle that I had.

In the week of the show he used the tactic of water manipulation, which meant I was drinking up to 12 litres of water a day till three days out from the show then I would decrease the amounts, so that on the final day I would just sip water. The idea is to fool the body into thinking it has too much water and you have to urinate more often, well not just more but at times it felt constant. This was okay but a little embarrassing, having to say to customers "excuse me" all the time. I even had to carry a number of two-litre empty milk cartons to use to and from work. This became an essential piece of kit to help me covertly make the many pit stops I had to take. It isn't easy to sit there with your penis inside a big milk jug covered only by your coat while trying to look nonchalant, but it was far better that using the pint containers I had previously used.

It was certainly a learning curve trying to disguise that tell-tale sign that you pissed yourself. I remember one of my mates who delivered for a very well-known leaflet company once told me he used to pray that people weren't in so that he could gain access to the rear of their property and have a sneaky piss.

The worst part for me was he had me "carb up" which is to eat more carbohydrates to ensure the body is full of glycogen. Most bodybuilders relish this part of the regime, but for me it meant forcing food into my already shrunken stomach and worse still I hated loads of potatoes, but Ben had made out the plan and I was going to stick to it.

I had 15 medium baked potatoes to eat the first and second day and I had to stay up until 12 o'clock to eat them, not that I got much sleep anyhow as my trips to the toilet had me contemplating if it may be a good idea to get a pillow and kip next to the bog.

The day before the show, my friends helped me with the ritual of shaving and tanning up. It always felt good to see that colour go on, in fact in some ways it felt like an artist adding the final touches to his latest painting.

I knew one of my opponents for the competition, Gary, because he used to come into the shop a lot. His favourite trick was to drop his baggies just about anywhere; I think half of Manchester had seen the great "wheels" he had.

We arrived at the venue in Dudley early as usual due to my paranoia about being late. Dudley at nine o'clock in the morning isn't exactly a centre of activity and we had to walk a fair way to find a coffee, but to my amazement I wasn't the only "weirdly" tanned looking alien to land in Dudley. Others had descended already and the local inhabitants regarded the "alien species" with open-mouthed amusement.

The venue was a well-used one. The curtains were tarnished and the hall looked as though in its day it had been a fine setting for all sorts of events, but now it looked tired and its floors creaked under the weight of the massive people that trod its stage. Backstage at competitions is a surreal world as you will find people lying on the floor with their legs in the air, trying to relax, and others nervously pacing the floor, flexing their arms and doing "the walk" in the vain hope they are intimidating the opposition.

I took a supplement called niacin for the first and only time and took my time eating chocolate and having a swig of whisky. I was ready and started pumping up, my veins jumping out with the effect of the whisky and niacin starting to hit!

It is a strange effect that dieting has on you as you become so focused on the competition that you don't let anything else distract you. Backstage is usually segregated into men's and women's changing rooms, but not always. Getting ready to go on were the female fitness competitors, who posed and strutted in front of me and the guy who was rubbing some oil on my back. Well he started off rubbing oil on my back and then sort of went off into his own little world and stood two feet away from me, his hands making non-existent contact but still maintain a rubbing motion, while he stood gawping open-mouthed at the line-up of beautiful women in front of us.

There were about 26 contestants all vying for the title, it was such a big line-up, and we had to be brought out in two ranks. All the guys were pushing for room and I learnt quickly that I would have to fight to ensure that I could be seen. My elbows became my space-finders but as Ben had told me, always smile, no matter what. So with this hideous grin on my face, I nudged the guys to my left and right and went through my compulsory poses.

It was hot as hell on that stage and luckily for us all there were very few call-outs. My number was called in rounds one, three and four and just as I was beginning to feel the pace, the MC shouted like a film director giving the order to cut. "Please give these guys a round of applause and you'll see them tonight."

It felt like there should have been a lot more comparisons given the size of the line-up. I don't know if all the guys got a call-out, it seemed like it had been cut short like someone had suddenly taped the finishing line at the ten-mile marker during a marathon race, but all I could feel at that moment was relief that it was all over.

I stayed on to watch my friend Paddy compete in the tall class and because he was impressed how the niacin had made me so vascular, he decided to use some too. Paddy always did things to the extreme and although he knew I had used two, he became very grandiose and reckoned because he was bigger, he would need six. The last thing I saw before he went on stage was that the niacin had made him vascular alright, in fact there was a massive vein throbbing in the middle of his forehead and he was saying in his Geordie twang that he was "hot man, very hot"!

He looked unsteady as he posed and when he came backstage to await his free round, he looked worse. He looked really ill, veins were sticking out everywhere and he looked like he had just stepped out of a sauna. He was gasping for water and I handed him a bottle. He was drinking like a guy who had been lost in a desert for a week, splashes were going over his tan, but he seemed not to notice, his eyes looked distant and he didn't even hear his name being announced for his individual round.

We had to prise the bottle off him and prompt him back on stage; well we sort of had to push him. He staggered back on stage like a drunken man and only started posing when the music had been on for a few seconds. He posed to 'I Believe I Can Fly' and at the end he suddenly dropped to the ground and fell to his knees. I immediately thought: "Shit, he's passed out!"

I nervously looked at the fire exit. Was he dead? Would I be made responsible, because I had given them to him?

Should I make a run for it? All of this passed through my mind in a flash! I was the most relieved person in the place when he did eventually rise, although somewhat shakily, to his feet.

The sudden "drop" that he had executed like an elephant that had been shot, I later found out, was meant to be a graceful flowing move, but he had nearly blacked out and needed to make an emergency landing. Thankfully I wasn't being interrogated by the police because Paddy was still with us, definitely the worse for wear, but still alive and after he was feeling a bit better. He joined me, Ben and some friends as we vacated the hall and went off to find a local fast food café to waste a few hours and to have something nice to eat.

Gary was in there too and the talk came around to who we thought had taken the title. It was agreed by all that me and Gary were in the first three but it was close, very close.

At the night-time show the place was packed, the atmosphere electric and thunderous applause greeted us as we stepped back on the stage. It is an amazing feeling to walk on the stage in front of hundreds of people in the best shape of your life. We went through the mandatory poses, then a few token call-outs and then finally the MC shouted "pose down" and 26 competitors ran for the best spot on stage but I was nippy, I got there first, directly in front of the judges and just as I started to hit my favourite poses I realised that the momentum of the other competitors wasn't stopping and I was knocked within an inch of falling off stage.

In bracing myself, though, I had developed a problem: my hamstring was in knots, it was killing me and the worst thing was that Gary was now alongside me and I had to put everything into the posing and hit the hams regardless of the pain.

Pose after pose we hit, cheesy grin after cheesy grin until after about four minutes of absolute hell, they told us to go to the back of the stage. There were six of us left after the others collected their medals for competing and then it was down to the last two. I couldn't believe what was happening; it had come down to me or Gary to take the title. The MC seemed to take an age but eventually he announced that Gary had taken the title and I was second.

I felt deflated as if someone had unplugged me from the socket of adrenaline I had been riding on. I stood there and smiled as the photographer took his shots. I saw Gary taking centre stage and I knew that he had only beaten me because of the massive development of his quads. It is a strange feeling being on stage in second place, you don't know whether to celebrate or to feel a certain amount of disappointment. Some people call second the first loser spot and I guess in a way as I stepped off the stage, I felt to some degree that the season had ended on a low, but if you would have told me at the qualifier in Doncaster that I would end up second, I would have ripped the trophy out of your hand there and then.

As I got backstage and started to wipe some of the oil off the heavily stained tan, I was more determined than I had ever been. I didn't want to be second again, but I had to improve. Targeting the quads and hamstrings would be a priority, but now the season was drawing to a close and Christmas was looming for most people. For me in the frame of mind that I felt at the time, it wasn't a time of celebration, it was an inconvenience and it would mess with my workout schedule.

Taking time out

I DECIDED to take 1998 off as I knew with my present physique that it was going to have to improve if I was going to do better. I was also learning more about gear and combinations and although I was no longer feeling faint when I injected, I still disliked the feeling of sticking a needle in my butt.

My mind was really focused and I found that even some of the bigger guys were avoiding training legs with me. If I didn't feel sick or couldn't move, it felt like I hadn't done enough. I was maxing out with five-a-side on the free squat, concentrating hard on the depth and movement of every rep. Workout partner after workout partner went into meltdown, I would see a guy I knew working quads and go up to them and ask if they wanted to train with me and some would either cry out or say they had finished. I was an addict and everything outside the gym seemed to be an obstruction.

I found that my times off the gear left me feeling depressed and it was one of these times that I found myself seriously thinking about my life. It used to take me nearly an hour a day to get to work in the rush hour and I knew that those wasted hours could be utilised to greater effect in the gym. I was beginning to hate the travelling and I had no patience to talk to newbie guys about training so I found myself repeating the same dribble every day. I was going stir crazy and if one more punter asked me why they needed to use protein, after me talking to them for more than half an hour about the subject, I would have probably have not been responsible for my actions. I could see the headline: "Steroid Rage; Assistant manager assaults customer with tubs of whey protein"! I knew that I had to move on. Things were changing at the place I was working, the shop was closing and the warehouse was being relocated.

It was an advert in the *Bolton Journal* that caught my eye. I was looking for something new, something that would allow me to train, be close enough to a gym and didn't wear me out. The post was for a person to train as an outreach worker to visit people with mental health problems in the area of Bolton. Once again, like a candle in the wind, I ended up completely changing my direction in life. It wasn't because I had found a new vocation, as I told the new company that employed me, it was because it was local to where I lived and my idea was to eat, train and work in Bolton, so that all my energies could be concentrated on getting bigger.

I started my new job as a mental health trainee support worker with Creative Support in Bolton. I hadn't a clue about the job, but it just seemed that all you had to do was talk to people and I could do that and it wasn't manual work and therefore wouldn't interfere with my training.

The new gym that I found was in a back street in Bolton and a mile and a half from my home, called Bodyzone. It was owned by natural champion Kevin Alder and it was my kind of gym, filled with guys hungry and striving to be bigger. It was hardcore and basic, no fancy machines here. You could sense the atmosphere the moment you stepped inside, this wasn't a gym for the posing crowd. It was just like O'Malley's, filled with adrenaline, testosterone and screams of desperation and pain.

I felt totally at home from the moment I started training there. It psyched you up watching the other people smashing out the reps aggressively. People didn't avoid me here, they recognised that I was a competitor and wanted to train with me; it was open warfare. I wanted to beat them and they wanted to beat me!

I remember once being given a supplement called GABBA by one of the guys before we "beasted" the quads. We had done sets at four and five plates, when Kevin said: "Let's rep out on three plates a side." In layman's terms this means go until you can't do another rep. This is fine with most exercises but with quads it's a killer, your breathing goes and then your legs turn to jelly. I think the guy we trained with, Tony, got 20, Kevin got 30 and me who had taken the GABBA that makes you invigorated and ultra competitive got under the bar and smashed out 20 reps. My breathing was hard and fast but I closed my eyes and squeezed out another ten reps. My head felt like it was going to pop, but on wobbly legs I pushed out another two.

I collapsed on the floor after securing the bar and could see the guys looking really worried. I couldn't get my breath, I felt faint and nauseous, I could feel the darkness surrounding me and then nothing. As the shadows lifted I could feel someone shaking me and I remember thinking that I was a kid at home and had overslept and my dad was trying to wake me. Then as I opened my eyes I woke with a start! Into my view came Kevin and then I realised that I was not sleeping, I had passed out. I could see Kevin's mouth moving, but no words. Expecting some sympathy I looked at him and then his words reached me: "Don't die here mate, it'll give the gym a bad reputation, we thought we'd have to roll you out into the car park for a minute there!"

Leg sessions at Bodyzone were always memorable. Lee, a young chap who was looking to compete for the first time, was training with me and Kevin on one occasion and we were really smashing it. You would do your set, fall to the floor exhausted while the other two did their sets or spotted and then you had to get back up in time to batter your quads even more.

It was when I was "spotting" Lee, which means I was directly behind him and there to give him support if he got in trouble. We had five plates aside on the bar and Lee got under and started to growl aggressively before standing up with the bar straining over his shoulders. I heard him take a sharp breath then he descended slowly until he was beyond parallel. He was grunting with the effort, but then he started the lung-busting journey to stand up again. He repeated this and I could feel he was giving everything and then it happened just as he was coming up on the third rep.

I heard this "oh fuck" followed by this moan. I staggered back with him, supporting the bar, thinking he had hurt himself, but no sooner had we racked the weight back safely than Lee started this half-skipping, half-running movement right past me. He wasn't in pain, he was rushing straight to the toilet. Then the awful smell hit me. He had done the dreaded follow-through that is an occupational hazard of hardcore training. He timed it beautifully though and had wiped, cleaned himself up and come out again, just in time for his next set!

The job, after a few weeks shadowing other members of staff, required me to go into the homes of people with different mental health problems and to do holistic therapeutic work with them.

I had heard of schizophrenia before, but likened it to Jack Nicholson's character in *The Shining*, so it was with some trepidation I got my first service user to work with. He was an Asian chap who had paranoid schizophrenia and I was told in simple layman's terms that when he was ill he imaged things.

The second time I visited his home he was brushing his carpet and clouds of dust were enveloping the air. Gasping for air I asked if he was okay as he seemed irritated and he stated that in the flat upstairs, the people were hammering and banging all day. I listened, there was no noise at all and I made the stereotypical mistake of not undertaking further investigation.

I called his CPN and stated that I thought he was becoming paranoid. He requested that I keep observations up and to report back to him if this became a "fixed" idea. As I arrived the next morning, I noticed that there were workmen on the roof of the flats and that the noise he was hearing was real and nothing to do with paranoia and the real problem was an inexperienced worker.

Taking the title

IN LATE 1998 I began making plans with Ben to compete in two Open British championships, the EPF and WABBA events. Training was going well at the Bodyzone. Kevin, who owned it, was as dedicated as I was and we had some brutal workouts together, but there was always fun and in one instance, I got to do some extra work in *Hetty Wainthropp Investigates* starring Patricia Routledge because the gym had been picked as a location spot.

It was my one and only experience of acting and maybe it was because the storyline was about a gym owner supplying steroids that I felt stereotyped already. I couldn't believe how hard acting was and for one scene I was leg-pressing about four plates a side in the background as the real actors played out their roles. Leg-pressing with that weight wasn't hard for me, but by the 20th re-take my quads were seizing up and the strain depicted in the drama is definitely real. Unknown to me, Kevin and the other guys had set me up. Apparently most of the re-takes weren't needed after all.

Due to unforeseen circumstances, we also had to find a new supplier of gear mainly due to our old supplier going on a temporary vacation at Her Majesty's Pleasure. We arranged to meet the chap at this swanky pub in Manchester. He informed us that we could meet in the main car park, but to be aware that the pub was a "Hooray Henry" type and to try not to look out of place. Me and my mate wore suits and ensured we took his car because it was more upmarket than mine. We waited anxiously for the guy to arrive, when this rickety old car whose exhaust was making a right racket pulled up near us and this giant of a man emerged from this small Fiat like Houdini escaping a shackled sack. He was wearing the brightest baggies and sweatshirt and seeing our car, shouted at full blast: "Hey lads, sorry I'm late."

The eyes of people sat outside drinking were drawn to him like Blackpool Illuminations. It was made even more suspicious by me and my mate trying to fit into the close confines of this guy's little Fiat and him putting the vials of gear we were buying on top of the dashboard of his car. I told my mate that we couldn't have been more blatant if we had put an advertisement in the local paper: "Come and see Bodybuilders buying gear at XXX pub, tonight at 7.30, everybody welcome!"

It was strange how open most people were about selling gear. It was almost like they thought it was legal and I think part of the reason for that is that gyms, well some gyms, have been selling steroids so casually for years and only when you heard down the grapevine that someone had been nicked for it did you get slightly worried.

After he had taken his bows to the audience he had created, he left in his rickety old Fiat to the accompaniment of his exhaust executing an appropriate loud banging noise as his finale. I stood with my mate with two large bags of steroids and "our audience" now seemed to be studying our every move. I felt like a scarfed Manchester City supporter in the Stretford End as we got into the car, we were so obvious. That was the first and last time that we decided to get gear off him as it seemed that some people were questioning the quality of his sources and also because we had found another supplier that was more local and the quality seemed better, but most importantly, we wanted someone with a modicum of discretion because neither of us wanted to share our living quarters with a hairy-arsed cell-mate.

I was visiting a client who was well known to services and extremely strong. The last time he had been sectioned into hospital it had taken six policemen to subdue him. When I first met him, I had expected to meet a real aggressive guy who was built like Mike Tyson, but I couldn't have been more wrong. He was in fact a really nice guy when he was well and with his heavy black glasses, he resembled an older version of Harry Potter.

I had known him for a few weeks and we would go to the supermarket and do some shopping and have something to eat in the local café. Everything was going well until one morning, I arrived and his normally well-groomed hair looked ruffled. He let me in and proceeded to secure the front door with the three locks and then put the door chain on. This made me feel a little uncomfortable, but as I followed him into the living room, he began to pace up and down and he looked bemused.

I asked why he was so happy and he told me that he was thinking about the Yorkshire Ripper and how he wore nappies. I tried to keep calm and made light of it and asked how he knew the Yorkshire Ripper. He then replied that he was the Yorkshire Ripper and at this point went into the kitchen and I could hear cutlery being rattled. I went from being slightly concerned to feeling full-blooded terror, I could hear the chinking of the cutlery and all I could think was: "He's got a bloody knife, and I'm well and truly fucked!" I felt my heart beating like hell. The front door was locked, the windows were doubled-glazed and I was locked in the room with a man who thinks he's the Ripper.

I stood near the television, debating with myself if the Ripper ever attacked a man, but maybe if he did, nobody had ever found out? I could feel the hairs on the back of my head tingling, my mouth felt dry, but outwardly I was trying to look calm as I lingered near the television set. He was in the kitchen for what seemed to be minutes but I guess it was shorter and then I heard his footsteps coming back in. I had made up my mind that if he had a knife, I was going to try to bash him with the portable TV and now as I sensed him coming into the room, in anticipation, my shaking hands took their clammy hold on the portable.

I heard him saying something, and then he was suddenly there, right in front of me. I looked at his hands; was it the long bladed kitchen knife? No, it was a cup of tea being slowly stirred by a teaspoon. The cutlery I had heard being rattled was a teaspoon! I was safe; I felt the tension leaving my body and I have never been so happy to see someone drinking a cup of tea. I made my excuse to get him to open the door and phoned his CPN to get some assistance as he was still deluded that he was the Yorkshire Ripper and needed to be assessed for possible hospital admittance.

Before the main shows, my friend Big Kevin and I decided to do the 1999 Muscle Beech classic near Birmingham. I decided to experiment with diuretics. We arrived early and I spent the next few hours constantly using the toilets.

There were only four guys backstage for the novice event and looking around us, I thought it was between me and Kevin, but the MC came backstage and explained that they had to wait for another competitor as he was delayed in traffic. Now we both thought that was strange as bodybuilding shows never hold up an entire show just for one person, unless it was Dorian Yates of course, but eventually after over an hour this guy arrived.

Apparently he had just won some top event and I thought: "Well how come he is a novice then?" I sensed that something may not have been as it seemed. As you will no doubt know if you have ever competed, politics definitely have their place, but if this was some kind of subterfuge, then unfortunately for the conspirators things were not going to plan.

First, the guy arrived extremely late and then we got to see him stripped off and lo and behold in the few weeks between his win and this competition, he had definitely been pigging out. He wasn't cut and he was bloated with water. I was smiling to myself because I knew although he was bigger, he wasn't in shape to beat either of us.

When we walked on stage, they announced that the winner of the novice competition would be awarded this beautiful cut-glass bowl. It looked stunning, glimmering under the lights, and it certainly looked a thing of beauty and expensive too. I now felt confident that either myself or Kevin would be lifting that sculptured piece of glass as we posed next to each other. "Naivety in the face of bodybuilding politics," I call that moment.

The lights went down, which is weird as most shows have the lighting extremely bright to show up every detail of the bodybuilder. There is no reason why you would lower the light, unless of course you wanted to hide the quality of the physiques.

I was called out first, then Kevin, and then the guy we had been waiting so long for was called out to thunderous applause. He was an aggressive guy and was trying to shove us as we posed against him, but both of us stood our ground. I could hear people shout "show em!" to the crowd favourite. I could feel his elbows knocking into me but I was smiling the cheesy grin and no one was giving an inch. I hit the poses hard and I could hear the crowd favourite screaming with the effort of trying to pull out all the stops, but even under the soft lights, his body still looked soft and puffy.

In the individual rounds of posing my music was nothing short of diabolical. The music was so low I could hardly hear it and at first I stood there looking at the MC, thinking that they will sort out the problem and then I could start my posing, but he ushered me on and I went through the motions, to this insipid version of the song from *Pulp Fiction* played at a tenth of the volume it was meant to be.

I initially thought that it was probably a bad recording, until Kevin's rock music that normally shatters your ears came out sounding as low as mine did. We both looked at each other backstage and rationalised that maybe the sound system was messed up, but as I began to say something, I was rudely interrupted with this earth-shattering roar of rock music and on strutted the crowd favourite to a crescendo of hoots, whistles and roars. I looked at him as he posed, he still looked bloated and he was carrying body fat but under the low lights and to this torrent of noise, his size stands out.

I looked at Kevin as the music blurted out and I had to shout to be heard: "Looks like they found the volume button Kev!" It wasn't surprising when they announced me in third, Kevin second and guess what? The guy we had been waiting an eternity for won. I swear to this day that they had already engraved his name on the cut-glass bowl.

Feeling a bit gutted, I decided to do the pro-am as well because there was prize money. I didn't expect to win but we were there anyway. Kevin would tell you that he was reluctant and I spent ages persuading him, which is sort of true, but what really happened is he said no, then I mentioned it was for £1,000 prize money and I hadn't seen any of the top pros and suddenly he was in the changing rooms donning his posing gear quicker that Superman on speed!

When we got backstage, there were a handful of competitors and no one of any note. Every time the door opened, I expected that some well-known pro would walk in, but apart from a weary backstage guy shouting that we had five minutes until we were due on stage, no one else showed their face.

I could sense that even Kevin, who was reluctant to do the class, was getting fired up and as I was doing a set of dumbbell curls, I whispered to Kevin: "Are we going to split it mate?" He smiled and nodded "okay".

I could feel the adrenaline pumping, my confidence was high and I was grinning to myself. I was thinking to myself that this was going to be the biggest pay day of my career as the MC announced that all competitors for the pro-am should go to the side of the curtain and take their place in the line-up. Not every venue has two changing rooms, but to my horror this one had and looming through the shadows came another four guys. I saw the stage lights block them out before I actually could make out who they were, but Gary Lister, a well-known mass monster, was one of them.

I could feel my muscles deflating as I stood next to Gary. He was about four stones heavier than me and in shape. I had a plan though. I told Kevin that in the pose-down I was going to stand in front of Gary, so the judges couldn't see him. I've never been on any stage wishing I hadn't bothered, but as I stood next to the hulking frame of Mr Lister, all I could do was laugh at our predicament.

Kevin said afterwards that he was never going to listen to one of my "good ideas" ever again, but bodybuilding is full of surprises and although he kept his promise and didn't listen to one of my good ideas ever again, some years later, he took on Mr Lister in a heavyweight British final showdown and matched him for muscle mass.

Besides the odd adrenaline rush at work with clients, I was training hard for the up and coming EPF championships, but I was starting to detest the twice weekly injections into my arse. I loved what it did but hated the pain.

It was at this time one of my advisers introduced equipoise into my steroid regime. Apparently it would help harden me up for the forthcoming competition. He handed me the bottle and the first thing I noticed was that the box that it came in was highlighted by a picture of a beefy-looking bull. It stated that it was for "veterinary" use only and the doses it gave were for cattle, horses and bulls, but not for 14.5st humans.

I questioned him and said: "I can't use this, it's for animals, and I'm really worried about using it." His answer was from the bodybuilder's bible itself, he flexed his back and chest and stated: "What doesn't kill you will make you stronger," and then added the thought-provoking speech: "Listen Jim, they use this on thoroughbred horses that are worth millions, if it wasn't good shit, they wouldn't risk it would they?"

I don't know if it was the lack of food but at the time I remember thinking that was a pretty logical statement as he helped me inject it into my deltoid muscle. I don't know if there were side-effects to the drug but I remember thinking: "If I start neighing or chasing sheep I'm coming straight off this stuff."

The week before the show, something felt wrong; the injection spot on the right hand side of my arse was sore, very sore. I was feeling feverish and as the days went on, it started to get swollen. I used ice and tried to massage the spot but it just felt worse. I couldn't sleep properly and at one stage, I had to prop my side up off the mattress to get any respite from the pain.

I thought about seeing my doctor but I feared that she would put me on a course of antibiotics like the hospital had done with a friend of mine. I was only a day away from my show and I figured that any medical intervention would affect my preparation so although I had over 200 miles to travel that day and I could feel my body becoming ravaged with some kind of fever like I was coming down with flu, very gingerly, I seated myself in my mate's car and started the journey south.

I was glad that most of it was on the motorway because I could feel every bump, pot hole and crevice in the road and the epicentre of pain was my arse. I often contemplate that nowadays I wouldn't have taken such a risk and that I would definitely have sought the advice of a doctor, but I was younger then and my mind never questioned my own mortality for one moment.

When we all arrived at the Travelodge at Halesowen, it was a lovely summer night as we made our way into the reception area to check in and we all arranged to meet in the bar later on.

I was feeling increasingly edgy about the competition and when I got into the confines of my room, I knew I had to get out of there and try to take my mind away from how ill I felt. I wandered around the grounds, alone in my thoughts and I ended up going into the bar early as I was bored and needed to sit down.

It was filled with mostly businessmen who chatted away to each other and they barely made any eye contact with me as I bought a glass of diet Coke and looked for a secluded spot away from everyone.

It was then I spotted a familiar face. Simon was there, his huge frame highlighted by the glow of his orange false tan. He was a good friend and I had dined with him and his family on various occasions. It was great to see him. He hadn't told me that he was competing but as I approached him, he looked at me strangely, like he didn't know who I was and then I realised why. Sat opposite to him and slightly obscured by one of the stone pillars in the room, was a rather attractive, younger lady, who wasn't his wife. I hesitated, but it was too late, she had already noticed me, there was no way back, despite the pleading look in his eyes. I looked at him and said: "Hi pal, what you doing around here?" "Hi Jim," he replied. "I'm competing tomorrow."

The lady he was with coughed as though she was saying: "Aren't you going to introduce him to me?" He looked sheepish and said: "Oh yes and this is Mary, my er, friend." I shook her hand and smiled. "I can't believe he's brought his bit on the side to a competition," I thought. I could sense the tension in his voice and he may have been smiling but his eyes said "fuck off Jim". But the lady he was with pulled out a chair and beckoned for me to sit down. She told me they were just friends and she had come with him to help him with his tan.

They were drinking wine and she poured me a glass. I was feeling rough but decided to accept the drink as I thought it might relax me a bit. Several glasses later, she was a bit worse for wear and was behaving more and more intimately with him. He looked like Basil Fawlty as his body language was trying to deflect any sexual attention she was offering. She, however, was now looking at him with these big blue eyes, lovingly watching every gesture he made, while he was like a rabbit caught in the car headlights. It was so obvious something was going on but even when she went to the loo he denied that she was anything but a friend.

I walked back to the rooms with them and I couldn't believe it as he hesitated and said: "This is my room." It was next to mine. He gestured for Mary to go to her room, but she was now too drunk to understand this subterfuge. She clung to his arm and was staggering. He looked at me and was still trying to blag the situation. "I think I'll let her sleep on the sofa," he said. I couldn't have cared less because by now I was feeling so hot because of the fever and the wine that I just wanted to sleep.

I said my goodnights and just went in my room, got undressed and fell on to the bed. I was so hot that I just lay there, naked, looking up at the ceiling. My thoughts drifted to the competition the next day and the pain in my butt, but this was rudely interrupted by the sounds of passion rising from next door. It was either passion or that sofa that she was supposed to be sleeping on was so bloody uncomfortable. As the night went on she was wailing like a banshee. Despite this interrupting any sleep that I might have got I was well impressed by his stamina, particularly before a show.

The next morning at breakfast was slightly embarrassing. I sat there with my friends as they both came down the stairs. Now I know I looked rough because of the fever and all the dieting, but he looked like death warmed up. I couldn't help myself and shouted to him: "You sleep okay?" "On and off," he replied. I thought to myself: "I know you were bleeding on more than off last night."

She meekly said: "I didn't sleep much either, I think I was excited." I said: "I heard you moaning a bit, bet that sofa was uncomfortable?" She never replied and just looked away as me and my mates tried to hide amused smiles.

My friends were still urging me to go to the hospital but all that I could think was I hadn't gone through all this not to compete now. I convinced them that I would go and seek medical attention as soon as the show had finished.

As we arrived at the venue, I could barely sit down and the preliminary introductions of the MC passed me by as sweat rolled down my fevered body. I could hear my friends chat, I don't know if it was to me or about me and at that stage, I didn't care as I felt my mind drifting in and out.

I felt a little better when I saw Simon on stage looking fucked. Literally! After the first few call-outs, his body slumped and he couldn't hold the poses. I was screaming for him to hold it tight at the back of the stage, but he was dead on his feet. He could hardly keep erect, no doubt because he had been erect all the previous night and now everything was wilting and not just his ardour.

He didn't place and he just gave me a thumbs-up as he met me backstage as I was setting my bag out. I smiled to myself and thought that only Simon would think of bringing his mistress to a show and shagging her all night before a major final.

There were only four competitors in my line-up, but I felt so bad that all I could do was to lie down backstage and stick a pillow under the swelling on my arse. It was lucky for me that with the tan and the way the trunks fitted, it disguised everything. I remember trying to pump up and slowly the adrenaline crept in and helped me start to make a half-baked attempt at warming up. I honestly felt that against the frenetic approaches of the other guys, I was in my own time warp, where I was going through exercises in slow motion.

It seemed an age before the haze lifted and I found myself on stage with three quality guys. The lights were not any hotter than usual but my feverishness was adding to the sickly heat I felt. It was lucky there were just four of us because my body was shaking with every pose that I struck and I knew I had little left.

After the mandatories, I was waiting at the side of the stage to do my 90-second free-posing routine, when a member of the St John's Ambulance crew came backstage and asked if I was okay. I knew I wasn't but thanked them for their care and assured them that I was alright. In the pose-down I could feel the strength ebbing from me. I was beginning to feel faint but somehow I kept on and to much applause I took the novice EPF British title.

I had never dreamed of taking a title, to me it didn't matter at what level. At that moment in time I thought of my old dad training me in the back yard, spending hour after hour helping me with my shot-putting. I recounted how my mum would argue with him about how muddy I got. I always had a wash after but we only bathed once a week when the boiler would be lit for all the members of the Moore clan. At times like this, everything was overwhelming.

I guess in the lead-up to competing you never allow yourself any time to think, you just know what you have to do and get on with it. You become like a machine, automatically eating the right fuel and churning out the reps and sets. Then after the show you become human again but now all I thought about was mum and dad and how I wished they were here to see me win.

The guys were going crazy and they wanted to go out and celebrate with me but by this stage, any elation I was feeling about winning was rapidly fading away and being replaced by agonising pain. The fever was getting worse and I knew I had to get out of there and get medical attention as soon as possible.

The wilderness years

I DON'T know if it was bravado or sheer adrenaline, but I managed to get out of the venue into my friend Helen's car and as I perched gingerly on the seat, my arse was throbbing as though I was sitting on barbed wire. She drove me all the way to Bolton and I hobbled into A&E.

I sat there with all the drunks, well I say sat, actually I couldn't sit even if they had paid me, but eventually after 20 minutes or so I got called in to see the triage nurse. I told her that I had sat on a nail as I didn't want a lecture about using steroids and I assumed that I would only need antibiotics like some of my friends who had similar experiences.

It was quite obvious to the nurse because I was muscular, had a shit-load of false tan on and my veins stood out all over my body like knotted chords that maybe I wasn't exactly telling her the truth and after some cajoling from the nurse about if I didn't tell her the truth they might not be able to give me the right treatment, I finally admitted it had been through injecting steroids.

I returned to wait with Helen, still assuming that the problem was insignificant and I would soon be on my way home. As we chatted, I offered to treat her to some lunch the next day for driving me to the hospital. It would be an agonising three more hours before I saw the doctor and his diagnosis would mean that Helen had to wait a number of months before she got the lunch that I promised.

The doctor informed me that I had an abscess that needed an immediate operation. I was in shock; they told me that if I waited any longer I would have developed septicaemia. It dawned on me that I had been stupid to take such a risk.

I was nervous as they led me to a bed that stated "nil by mouth".

Great, I thought, 20 weeks of dieting and now the hospital was starving me too. I lay there in the bed thinking how life certainly can be up and down. A few hours ago I had been wallowing in my triumph and it had truly been one of the best days of my life, now I was here strategically positioned on my good side with an electric fan sending wave after wave of cold air on my fever-laden body for company.

I wasn't left with my thoughts for long, they were interrupted by a porter and nurse who had come to take me for my surgery. The operation was a success and I awoke feeling groggy on morphine and the first thing that I saw through my clouded vision was that the bed was badly stained. The thought flashed through my mind that I was lying in someone's "used" bed. And then a cruder image had me thinking that I had shit myself. Or maybe it was blood, but then it filtered through my fog-like brain that the mess was through the false tan that I was still wearing.

I think the nurses were fascinated by the guy who was stained dark orange and looked like an anatomy chart, but unluckily for them they had inadvertently put me next to a guy who worked out at the same gym as me. Now the chat among bodybuilders, though fascinating to the iron clan, is exceedingly boring to others and from the very first few minutes, we chatted non-stop about bodybuilding. In fact he had a similar operation to me and I couldn't help but feeling that he had probably used the same product, but I don't remember anything on the label that said "inject me for a week's stay in hospital".

I was allowed no food until the following morning. The waft of breakfast greeted my nostrils and unlike my fellow patients who appeared very picky, I was ravenous. I ate my breakfast and I also scavenged leftovers from the others on the ward. At visiting time, my brother brought some money for me and the lady came around with the trolley for papers, sweets and other goodies and like a kid in a toffee shop, I went sugar crazy. The trolley lady must have thought that I was nuts as I would ask her how much I had left until I had spent the entire five pounds right up to the nearest penny.

It was four days before I got home. I think by that time the attraction of having a tanned muscular guy had faded just like my tan and the nursing staff sent me home on crutches and told me get as much bed rest as possible. I had to go the clinic every day to have my wound repackaged and for the first few days this was okay, until they discovered why I was still feeling feverish. The nurse who was doing the bandaging was asking me how I felt as I was bent over semi-nude and she was putting a substance similar to seaweed on my wound. I was burning up with fever and fortunately for me, she saw this and left me in a very precarious position to pass on her concerns to the doctor.

He eventually came to see me and after a brief examination, he informed me that they would have to increase my antibiotics. Now this was both news to me and my brother and we both exclaimed and in chorus: "What antibiotics?" It became apparent that the hospital had made a slight error and not provided them for me. From then on I was ordered to have total bed rest and they arranged for a community nurse to visit me and change my dressings at home.

It was tough being bed-bound. I found myself tensing my physique to see if it was still there. I would lie there bored out of my skull and start to pump my biceps by curling my arms up and down. It was the only way that I could amuse myself, well the only way I'm going to tell you about that is.

It was depressing lying in bed, watching the same old trivia on television. Daytime programmes are definitely for the masochist. It was the days before Sky so we only had five channels of rubbish compared to the hundreds of channels of even more crap that are aired as entertainment today.

My brother and friends came around so I wasn't short of company and most people would bring me treats and I went from eating six to eight meals of healthy food to dining in on white Magnum ice creams. I could see my stomach thickening and my body shrinking and I began to get withdrawal symptoms from the gym. I craved feeling the pump of my muscles and seeing the veins pop when I flexed them, but I had to keep the weight off the wound so it could heal.

The only time I forgot about it was watching Manchester United defeat Bayern Munich in the final of the European Cup in the last few minutes. I leapt out of bed and shouted with delight as Ole scored and then realised I couldn't stand up and went sprawling on the floor.

It was frustrating as the weeks dragged on. I was binging on junk because I was bored and depressed, my stomach was getting fatter and I was so knackered that even trying to hobble around the house or trying to make something to eat was a major chore. I wasn't the best of patients. In fact I was totally impatient and after a few weeks, I would wait until no one was around and try to do simple exercises such as close-grip press-ups, dips between chairs and free squats. I would be covered in sweat and shaking and then like a scene from Lou and

Andy from *Little Britain*, I would hear someone opening the front door and scramble back into my bed before they spotted me.

It was over six weeks before I could set foot in the gym again and I found that the weeks of incapacity and having to cold turkey the gear once again had reduced my strength and although my weight had increased, it was mainly around my mid-section. I had to re-educate myself again and my gung-ho nature had to be put on the back burner for the time being. Mentally I thought that my body was ready for an all-out intensity session but physically I knew that it would have to be rebuilt and my first few sessions back in the gym were definitely dismal excuses for work-outs but I was glad to be back and knew that I would slowly have to build up the momentum.

One of the most frustrating times for any athlete is the first few weeks back from injury when you are re-acquainting your body with the weights and for the first few sessions I was merely saying: "Hello, how do you do?" It is tough to the point of aggravating, but it has to be done right. If you rush it, in all probability you end up with an injury. In some ways it's like starting again, but most people say the difference is "muscle memory". This is a theory that your body can restore muscle tissue quicker than it can create new muscle, once the desired stimulus is given.

It was mental agony though to fight with weights that I had previously easily repped out with and as the weeks went by, I contemplated if whether muscle memory had developed amnesia. Session after session I hung in, knowing that the intensity would return and after a few more weeks, I could feel my muscles waking up again and dilating with the increased muscle flow only the iron can give. It is an awesome feeling. Arnie described it as "like cumming"! I have to agree as in some ways it probably does feel like an orgasm.

In bodybuilding, only the two extremes of highs and lows seem to exist with very little in between, but when you have finished a great workout and pushed yourself to the limit, no matter how tired you are, you feel invincible. Your muscles bulge with blood and you have that incredible feeling that you're alive and healthy.

I was beginning to feel everything returning. My physique was hardening again and I was chomping at the bit, I wanted to see that granite-like reflection greeting me back in the mirror. I had made up my mind that due to the trauma my body had been through my next competition would not be as a novice but in the masters category against guys who had competed for most of their lives. I decided that my next show would be two and a half years away because I was going to have to put more size on and the only way that I could do that was to be consistent in the gym and not interrupt my schedule with dieting for a show.

I also knew that I would have to get back into cycling the gear, but I had a few problems. The first was physical, I only had one good buttock to inject into, and the second was psychological, as the abscess had made me wary of using the gear again,

I knew by now that it was nothing to do with poor injection protocol because other people had similar problems to me and now I was suspicious of the environments that the new breed of underground labs were using to make steroids. It had become evident that some were being made in very unsanitary conditions. Gear had become a massive industry and these "pop-up" labs were out to make a quick buck and had absolutely no regard for what, if any, procedures they took to ensure that the labs were germ-free.

I had come close to losing a limb and my tortured mind had replayed the whole incident over and over again and in lucid moments between dreams I had seriously questioned my own sanity about why I didn't get help earlier. I knew that I had no option but to use gear, it was one of the tools of my trade and I had no doubt that like any top tradesman I would have use of them soon. In fact, my "natural" phase ended after only eight weeks. I have to admit that I was craving to go back on the juice. I knew that although my body was slowly reclaiming some of the wasted muscle, the time to kick-start my season needed to happen sooner rather than later.

It was one of the most difficult experiences of my life when once again I filled the syringe up with the discoloured yellow solution and knew that I was about to revisit the scene that nearly led me to seriously damage my health. I held the liquid to the light, watching the bubbles slowly being extinguished from the syringe, in a ritual that I had long become accustomed to.

The room felt chilled. I don't know if it was just cold or it just felt that I was watching the roulette ball being tossed around the wheel, bobbling in and out of the multiple numbered slots, but in my case the roulette wheel wasn't numbered, it was divided into infected and sterilised as I pressed the needle against my clammy flesh. I felt like the newbie who had collapsed all those years ago as I closed my eyes and gritted my teeth as my fingers pushed the contents of the syringe into my body, but this time I didn't faint, I just froze as though time had stopped existing and thought: "Let it be okay!"

It is strange but after that first shot I was okay again. Maybe it was a mental barrier that I had to overcome but as the weeks melted into each other, I was back into full flow, the gains were coming thick and heavy, I was eating well and my training was going through the roof.

For months I was totally focused and running on existence mode. I would eat, work, train and sleep, until that is the team I worked with at Creative Support invited me out on a works do. At first I turned them down as I hadn't had an alcoholic drink in ages and I was so preoccupied at the time with my training that I felt I was letting myself down if I veered even slightly away from my goal. It was only through much harassment by several team members that I reluctantly got suited and booted and met the rest of the staff in a bar in Horwich, near Bolton.

Now my life has had a lot of these moments, where seemingly insignificant events meant a dramatic change. I had extreme tunnel vision at the time and was living virtually like a monk and apart from some brief interludes with a few distractions of the feminine kind, I hadn't got a place for a steady girlfriend, but that was all meant to change as I stared drunkenly into the mischievous eyes of the lady who was to become my life partner, lover and best friend.

Her name was Joely. She worked with me and from day one, I knew that I liked her humour; she would pass the wittiest or most sarcastic remarks as quick as a fencer uses his sword to disable someone. Over the weeks I had known her she had me in hysterics even when I was the brunt of one of her comments, but if someone had a bad day, was feeling down or needed help or advice, hers was always the first shoulder to lean on. She was the complete opposite to me. She wasn't into bodybuilding and I found that refreshing. Now she will say that it was me who asked her out, but although I'll admit that I was drunk at the time, I distinctly remember her asking me to go out to a nightclub with her, so in my opinion she seduced me.

I will never forget our first date. Anyone who knows Bolton will know it's like the Wild West on a Saturday night and it wasn't any different as I went into the local vodka bar to wait for Jo. I had to make a smart re-adjustment as two doormen were trying to eject this guy through the door and then his friend started to throw chairs, but it all settled down as I got my drink of vodka and orange and stared aimlessly at the pub across the road, idling the minutes away until Jo was due to meet me.

My thoughts were rudely interrupted as all sorts of mayhem kicked off and about 15 guys came out of the pub in front of me and started knocking crap out of one another. It was like watching some documentary on television as I became an accidental voyeur of the scene being played out in front of me. As fast as it began, like a magician waving his wand, they all disappeared as the sirens of the police shrieked their nearness. I looked at the clock as Jo arrived, smiling and looking beautiful. It was 7pm and I thought to myself that if the evening was anything like the last 30 minutes it was going to be extremely interesting indeed.

It was as well. I found Jo's company just like the vodka, it was intoxicating and throughout the night, we were chatting as if we had known each other all our lives. Although as I had said before that Jo wasn't really sporty, she had this altruistic personality that meant even if most people thought we were chalk and cheese, she shared my dreams and understood why my sport meant so much to me. Don't get me wrong, she kept my feet on the ground, just because we were an "item" now didn't stop her from much mischievous teasing.

I knew after a few months of seeing Jo that I was developing strong feelings for her, but in the back of my mind I was scared because she was over 12 years younger than me and I had been hurt before, but life seemed to be throwing us more and more together.

I don't know who asked who to live with them, but I guess we just sort of drifted into it. We took temporary shelter at one of Jo's friends' houses in Bury and we rented it on a week by week basis until she wanted it back. In retrospect it was frightening, we had very few possessions and no real foundation to build on, but as time has gone by, she has always been there for me. She has been my soul, my heart, my raison d'être. I have always been the one who has been celebrated, the one who has been honoured, while Jo has stood silently in the background, adopting the many roles of chef, nurse, psychologist, psychiatrist, lover, but most importantly, my best friend.

Enough of this though, I don't want to polish her halo any more and besides she'll only expect some of the royalties if this book ever gets published.

As I previously said life was moving on for us both. Jo and I had both gained places on the DIPsw course at Salford University which meant that not only did we live tougher, we also studied together. Well I studied while Jo messed around and then had the cheek to get me to help her with her assignments. I would painstakingly plan each essay and spend weeks researching it and Jo would start hers with only three days left to the hand-in date and that was only after much prompting from me, but the discouraging part was that despite her poor preparation, her marks were always superior to mine.

I also had a new part-time job that meant travelling to Tameside. It was an exciting project working with homeless people who had other issues as well. It was also eye-opening. I met a chap called James who had been a wealthy businessman, but was now an alcoholic living in homeless accommodation. I remember seeing his hand shaking as he poured himself yet another drink of vodka and he told me how he once had a wife, kids, cars, nice house and thriving business. His wife had divorced him because he spent all his energy working, he started drinking, lost his licence and ending up losing everything. I had always had a stereotypical idea of people that were homeless, now I knew it could happen to just about anyone.

Silvers was the local gym, located above the town's mortuary, which I suppose is convenient in our sport if you overdo it and have a coronary. It was full of history having once been owned by Rob Worthington, who had been one of the top amateurs in Britain and it had a great atmosphere to train in just like O'Malley's.

The place was full of bodybuilders who were hardcore and it was strange being in there and thinking back to the skinny guy who had been so intimidated walking into O'Malley's for the first time. From day one at Silvers I felt at home and soon made some good friends. The machines were the old Nautilus type, and the seats were ripped. The paint was chipped and worn, the carpet bare. It was also cold as hell in the winter and deadly hot in the summer but it had a beauty, a place where the addicted like me could fart, burp, scream and grind through our workouts without having to make excuses for our actions.

Silvers was full of characters, even its owner with his long blonde hair and tattoos looked like an escapee from the World Wrestling Federation. He trained with a guy called Tony who had won the heavyweights with NABBA. Tony was one of the nicest guys you could meet, but his Mohawk and tattoos covering his 6ft, muscular frame made most people very wary of him. He lived with his mum and dad who were quite elderly and Joe had told me that he had phoned him recently and his old ma had picked up the phone and relayed the message in her quiet, well spoken manner that: "Tony could not come to the phone as he was just having his shot of growth hormone."

Then there was Al, who was an up and coming young bodybuilder. He was massive as a junior and his approach left nothing to chance. He was just as focused as me and John and even trained on Christmas Day with us.

The notices on the walls epitomised the character of the place: "If you're fucking strong enough to lift the weights, you're strong enough to put them away."

I had to use new injection sites as now I only had the one good buttock to inject into. For some people, injecting into your thighs is probably easy, but not for me, my quads chose to go into extreme spasm each and every time I injected into them. It is strange as when I think back now, steroids were always a double-edged sword to me. When I was on them I hated using them, but then again when I was off them, I counted the weeks until I could add more muscle.

When a bodybuilder comes off a course of steroids he will use products such as Nolvadex, Clomid or HCT (pregnant women's urine) in order to try to restore his own body's natural level of testosterone. Low "test" is probably one of the main reasons that many bodybuilders become slightly depressed when they are off the gear. No doubt there is also a chemical reason too, but most guys know that when they come off a cycle, it's about trying to keep their gains and many become despondent that their strength and size tend to diminish during this period.

Everything was going really well until a young man in a Volkswagen Golf decided to use my vehicle to halt his. I never did find out if his car actually had brakes but I do remember seeing his eyes. He looked scared as he fought with his steering wheel. I don't recall much more, but witnesses said he was doing over 50mph when he lost control. I woke up in hospital with my Jo and two doctors beside me. They were doing observations on me; I just couldn't understand why I couldn't do simple things like touch my nose without nearly poking my eyes out.

I felt really shaky and they told me they would have to send me for x-rays on my neck and back. I was tired and seemed to be going in and out of consciousness. The movement of the trolley bed made me open my eyes and I could hear the staff muttering something to me, but I was having difficulty understanding what they were asking.

The x-ray room came into my view and I seemed to be there an age with only the mottled tiles on the ceiling for company. It was suddenly filtering into my befuddled brain that my head was in some kind of restraint and that they were checking to see if there was any damage to my neck or back.

I could see by Jo's face that she was relieved when eventually the x-rays came back and there was no evidence to suggest I had injured anything. The head and neck restraints were removed and then I lay there for what seemed an age. I kept asking Jo why we were still there, but she just said that they wanted to do some further checks as they had concerns that my reactions and movements during the observations that they had carried out were not what they expected. The two doctors returned and Jo's mum turned up too. The staff carried out further tests on my reflexes; I noticed Jo's mum looking quizzically at Jo.

All I knew was that people seemed concerned. I found out later that I had very limited reaction to any stimulus. A specialist was called for and after making his observations he gave me the news that they wanted me to remain in hospital, so that staff could monitor me and he would arrange for me to have a CAT scan.

I hated being in hospital. I will have to admit that I gave Jo some earache. I couldn't see why I had to be there, until they came with a wheelchair to take me for my scan. Now I am a stubborn bastard; I'll always admit that and I off-handily refused to use the chair. It felt insulting. I was okay, well so I thought. The moment I stood up was closely followed by my head turning to blackness and my body crashing to the floor.

It shook me up and it was slowly dawning on me that all was not well. I felt exhausted and nervous as the nurses helped me into the wheelchair and guided me into the CAT scan room. I was worried. while I laid down things seemed okay, but besides feeling weak, I felt dizzy sat in the chair. I can't remember how I got onto the scanning machine, all I remember were the loud bangs it made as I lay there wondering what the hell was wrong with me?

The next moment I was laying in my bed. Time seemed to flicker in and out and I lost all track of the hours and days, but I do know that Jo was there most of the time and although I knew she was concerned she never outwardly displayed it to me. That is Jo's nature, calm on the outside but paddling like hell underneath. She was there when the consultant visited my bedside. I must admit by this time, anxiety had become my new best friend. We stayed awake together and it visited me every time I slept.

The doctor appeared by my bedside one day and he delivered some good and bad news. The CAT scan, he informed me, was clear, but it seemed I had a condition called brain trauma and he did his best to assure me this would probably clear up, but it would take time. I was told that they were happy to let me go home later in the day, but I would be have to be monitored as an out-patient as a precaution.

Jo was like a Sergeant Major with me when I got back home. She and her mum helped me into bed and she wouldn't let me out of there. She took time out from her studies at Salford University and became my favourite nurse. The first night home was terrible, I couldn't sleep and I don't think Jo did either. She had even put me an empty coke bottle near my bed so I could use it to urinate in, but unfortunately for Jo she had also put a fresh bottle of diet coke next to me too, so I had something to drink during the night. Well my excuse will always be that I was disorientated, but somehow in the night, I guess that I got the bottles mixed up and it wasn't until I was woken by my Jo shouting "you dirty bastard", and I opened my eyes to see her spitting fluid on the floor, that I realised what had happened, but I guess diet coke and urine don't work too well as a cocktail!

It took many visits to the hospital and much resting until I was able to get up out of bed and even then I felt so weak. It was frustrating. After being a person who was always on the move, I was virtually housebound. I remember trying to wash up while Jo had gone out and woke up with a load of broken dishes around me because I had collapsed.

Weeks turned to months and I could feel my body was putting on a lot of fat through my immobility, but I was determined to get back and after many aborted attempts I took my first tentative steps outside on my own. I walked around the block, probably not more than half a mile, but I was exhausted, holding on to a lamp post for support, but all I could think as I breathed heavily was that I was going to get better, no matter what.

Little by little I increased my work around the house, but I had very little strength and that worried me. At times I got emotional because I felt so weak. One day, I managed to put a pole across two doors in the kitchen and tried to do a chin-up and the effort it took me to do just the one left me in a heap and I ended up punching a gaping hole in the door because I was that frustrated.

Athletes are not the most compliant of people. We spend our whole lives striving to be better, stronger, faster, so when we are in a position where our bodies are not functioning at the level we are used to, we find it difficult to accept it.

I had been progressing so well from the abscess and now it seemed I was even further back after all the effort of the last few months. The dark days visited from time to time, like some unwelcome relative at Christmas, and sometimes I will have to admit I felt my days of competing were well and truly over. I would do something fairly insignificant like clean the living room and wake up on the floor in a cold sweat because I had passed out.

To make matters worse I was surrounded by pictures, videos and trophies that were constant reminders of where I had been and now all that stared back at me was a fat, flaccid resemblance of me. I don't know if it was despair or to punish myself further, but I ended up doing stupid things that made me even worse like pulling my shirt up and looking at the protruding stomach that was my waistline and thinking back to the washboard abdominals that I used to have.

I learned to set myself small chores and to not look at what I couldn't do but what I had achieved that day. It's strange how we take everything for granted until one day it's taken away from us. I had always enjoyed the incredible feeling that repping out with a maximum weight gives you, now I was happy to do a few simple exercises at home.

I had to attend a medical in Manchester with the doctor that my solicitors had engaged for me, so he could look at any long-term impairment. He was an old style doctor who you could see had come from some sort of military background, I found his manner very overbearing and I had to tell him I wasn't happy with the way he was talking to me, but after he read out that I had a haematoma on the brain as a baby and had to have a life-saving operation that I was totally unaware of, I don't remember anything else but walking out with Jo.

I know he did some reaction tests with me, but mine must have been the slowest in history after that news. I asked my brothers and sister but they had no knowledge of it either. It was like I had never really known who I was and there was no way of finding out anything further due to the hospital not keeping records that far back.

I found it ironic that when I had to go for another CAT scan they asked me if I had any metal in my head due to it being magnetic and I had to say that I didn't know. They stared at me incredulously and I ended up having to explain the whole story to them before they arranged for me to have an x-ray to determine if I had a "clip" in my head, but at least that came back negative, and I wasn't a "Metal Mickey" after all.

I only realised afterwards that my previous CAT scan would have identified if my head was full of metal because I would have stuck to the inside of the machine faster than a drawing pin sticks to a magnet.

I was way behind with my studies at Salford University and even though they offered me the opportunity to re-take the year, my ability to be able to concentrate was impaired. I tried to read some textbooks but my heart was no longer in going back to university. The prospect of training to be a social worker had lost its appeal and my confidence in my own ability was at an all-time low and the prospect of returning to full time studies really stressed me out.

I was relieved when Jo brought up the subject and I was able to be open and honest about how I felt. She said that she would stand by me no matter what I decided. I was going stir crazy at home so I decided foolishly to try to go back to my part-time job before I had been advised. I had to drive to Tameside and just getting in the car brought me out in a sweat. My breathing was fast and I realised as my hands shook on the wheel just how much the accident had affected me psychologically. I wanted to get out of the car and run, but I knew I had to do this or forget ever driving again.

Every car seemed close to me as I drove. I could feel the waft of butterflies as they dispersed their nervous energy into the bottom of my stomach and by the time I reached work I was exhausted. I felt drunk as I staggered into the office to be greeted by my friends and for them to take a step back and question my judgement that I was fit enough to work. It must have somehow got back to the manager, because the next thing, he appeared like Zebedee from *The Magic Roundabout* and after a brief conversation, told me in no uncertain terms that I was to go home and only return when I was healthy enough. I knew he was right; I couldn't even drive home, never mind go out and support other people.

It would be another six weeks before I actually was able to go to work, but life is full of crossroads and when the manager found out that I had to give up my university course, he invited me to come and work full-time for him. It was a great opportunity for me and he even allowed me to come back on a graded return. A few weeks later, I was driving to work three days a week, though a little shakily at times, but my confidence and strength seemed to be recovering, even though I knew that I still had a long way to go to being anywhere near as healthy as I had been before my accident.

I had been back at work for two months, but I was still under consultation from my doctor. On my last appointment, a few weeks prior, he had given me strict instructions that I still needed to lay off any weight training as he advised me that just returning to work would be taxing enough. It was now over six months since I had lifted a weight. I was around 16 stone but I looked more like Billy Bunter than a bodybuilder.

It was soul-destroying watching my body decay before my eyes and it was in one of those moments that I decided to go against any medical advice and go to the gym. I have to confess that I told Jo that I had been given the go-ahead. I got some strange looks from the guys when I got to the gym. They were glad to see me and it was great to hear the banter, but some of my close mates were concerned because apparently I "looked rough as fuck"!

Any notion of competing didn't enter my mind at this stage, but I did feel like an addict must do awaiting his fix and I knew mine would soon come through feeling the glorious pump of the iron. I looked around me and saw the other guys grunting their way through their workouts. I wanted to be like them, well not exactly them, but I wanted to hit the weights with no fear like they were doing, but now I felt fragile and to be honest slightly anxious. But there was no going back; I looked at the sets of dumbbells that I used to use on my heavy set. The 120lb set looked back at me and all I could feel was a sense of fear that had never been there before.

I felt jittery as I reached for a pair of 30lb dumbbells and sat with them on my lap and hesitated. "Here goes, shit or bust," I thought as I shakily pressed them above my head.

Thoughts flashed through my mind: "Was the consultant right about me not being ready to train yet? Would I end up collapsing? Would I make a fool of myself in front of my friends?" "Fuck it!" I exclaimed out loud and I bit my lip in concentration and slowly lowered the weights off to my side and then swung them back above my head in completion of the first rep of flies.

My arms were shaking. I don't know if it was the stress of the exercise, the exhilaration that I was back in the gym or that I hadn't fainted, but it didn't matter, all that counted was that I was back to doing what I loved to do. I had a massive grin on my face as I lowered the dumbbells on my last rep. To the outside world it meant nothing, but for me that first set gave me hope that one day I would be able to train with the intensity I used to.

To be honest it was a crap session. I barely used more than my warm-up poundage and after 15 minutes I was an exhausted, shaking wreck. But to me it was a triumph, and I couldn't help smiling as I talked to the guys at the gym. Jo would probably tell it differently, she would say that when she picked me up later from the gym, I was shaking, pale and half dead.

As the weeks went on, my strength and health improved. I was now back to working full-time but for me, any notion about competing still seemed an age away. Although my family made reassuring comments that I looked well, their words fell on deaf ears, because I never judged myself as a normal middle-aged guy. In fact I detested the word "normal". What serious bodybuilder wants to look normal? We spend hours in the gym trying to look freakish, so any comparison to your average-looking guy is not what I wanted to hear.

I knew I had an over-hang of fat and could see early signs of middle-aged spread and at times I was beginning to lose faith. In darker moments, I even thought maybe this was how my life would be from now on. I wasn't happy though, it may sound egotistical or grandiose, but somehow it felt like watching a piece of art slowly decay.

I know most people have a stereotypical image of bodybuilding having a load of over-sized egotistical and vain people. It probably has and I know my previous comments about not wanting to be judged as normal will probably reinforce the idea too, but what most people don't know is that competitors have to take themselves to the limit in terms of sheer gut-wrenching workouts while existing on a calorific diet for eight to 16 weeks that most people would find hard to last a day on. We have such low body fats that our skin becomes virtually transparent and we push the barriers mentally and physically to pursue a physique that is as near to perfection as possible. Most of the guys who compete are amateurs. They don't do it for the money, they do it for the glory, and only a very few people make a good living out of being a professional.

There are many bodybuilders but if you go to most local or national shows you will see that there are only a few competitors and this is for a damn good reason. It is not just the physical aspect, there are the psychological issues too. Depletion is just that. It means survival, you don't have a life, and you exist from one meal to another, one work-out to the next. I have seen many start out on the journey and many hardcore guys and girls stumble and fall.

I continually questioned my own ability to make the quantum leap of changing from the medium intensity work-outs into the hardcore, all-out intensity of competition training. Just because I had done it before meant absolutely nothing. Sure, I had an advantage over a newbie, but every time you set out on the road to compete it's different. Your body changes, so do social and financial commitments and the only way you know if you can still compete at the same level is to simply do it.

I have to admit that I was scared. I had got back to a reasonable level of training and my health was improving, but would I relapse if I raised the intensity? I had a choice to make and I knew there was no sure-fire certainty of success, but either I continued plodding through training sessions, watching the older guys with their beer bellies talking about the weekend and how many pints they sank and accepted this was now my life too or I took a chance and went for it.

Weeks went by and I worried not just about competing, but taking gear again. Okay, I had no serious issues with it before, but now I had health problems and the other thing was broaching it with Jo and how she would feel. I have never been a person who planned things, I guess changes happen to me, rather than me being dynamic and making a decision.

It was around May 2002, when I wearily walked into the changing rooms after another exhausting workout. I still didn't feel great even though my body was at last feeling the sensation of a half-decent pump but standing and posing in the mirror, cut to ribbons, was this guy who I came to know as John.

Around him others grouped and at first I just ignored them and started to get changed. When he was posing, I could see he had a similar physique to mine, not freakishly muscular but ripped. I got closer and started talking to him and we got round to talking about his competition and I ended up telling him about some of the shows that I had done. I always remember he looked at me as though he thought I was joking, but I didn't blame him. By now I had improved a little, but I was still fat and nowhere near carrying the amount of muscle I used to have. We talked for ages about different shows and found we had a lot in common. John had two jobs, postman by day and doorman by night. As we chatted, it became apparent that he was a true Iron Warrior and as dedicated as anyone I had ever met.

His physique looked great but his face had that look of someone going to their own funeral. He looked absolutely knackered and when he told me how much food he was on for his cut, I understood why he looked like death warmed up. I was amazed that he even had the strength to hold down a conversation.

I don't know what happened in those 20 minutes that we were talking, but Jo says that she will never forgive John as it was he who put her through another ten years of supporting me with my life as a competitive bodybuilder. John inspired me so much. It had reawakened old memories and they lay heavy on my mind as I casually told Jo about meeting him.

She tried to change the subject but I guess my mind was elsewhere as I suddenly realised she was asking me a question. It suddenly dawned on me she was asking: "You want to compete again don't you?" Jo, as usual, had guessed what was on my mind and I was reluctant to express my desire as I knew from her eyes that she was frightened. My health was improving now and she just wanted me to be well. I ended up just nodding. It felt in some ways that I was betraying her, she had given me so much and now I was asking her for even more support. I could see in Jo's eyes that although she wanted me to continue with my dream, she was also worried about my health problems, but at the time I just wanted her to agree and I was relieved when she reluctantly said: "I guess I can't stop you, if it's what you want to do."

I remember jumping out of my seat and hugging her. Looking back now, I know that I was selfish and before you guys who are steeped in the iron as much as me say that I was merely doing what I was destined to do, in reality I wasn't just playing Russian roulette again with my life, but Jo's too.

The life of a partner or loved one who is involved with a competitive bodybuilder is never easy; it marginalises so much of your life together. At times you can't socialise, you eat separately simply because the food we eat is too bland for any sensible human being to eat and when you're competing, your idea of a conversation is to say "yes" now and again, such is the depletion in your cognitive ability to hold down a half-decent conversation. It truly is hard and many relationships either fail completely or are severely under strain during this period.

Jo once showed her work colleagues my pictures and they made the stereotypical remark about it must be nice to wake up next to someone with a body like that. She informed them that I went to bed with thermals on as my body fat was so low and as for anything physical happening, she told them I found it hard to even raise a smile, never mind anything else when I was so depleted.

This ain't no yuppie flu

I T WAS one thing saying I could make a comeback, and another thing actually achieving it. Something else felt wrong. I felt shattered all the time, not just through work or training, but even when I had woken up from a good night's sleep. Sometimes I didn't feel like getting up at all because my body felt so weak. As usual I just tried to push through everything, but the harder I pushed, the more acute my tiredness became.

I got to the stage that when I was having some sort of blackout Jo thought that I was having a kind of seizure. I ended up having to go on the sick because I was at times so tired that I would stay in bed for days. This went on for some months. I would get days when I felt things were going well again and have a period where I was back training and feeling well, but then all of a sudden I would just feel like someone had pulled the plug out and I had hardly any energy at all. I thought I was just being lazy and time after time, I tried to push through it.

My philosophy of if something is in your way just keep pushing until you get through it wasn't working. It was one of the most frustrating times in my life and at times I doubted my sanity.

I was eventually referred to a neurologist by my doctor. He was one of the country's leading specialists and even in the first meeting after he had listened to the health problems that I had, he stated that he didn't think I was experiencing epileptic fits. He arranged for many tests over the next couple of months to analyse my heart, brain and to also look at any chemical imbalances. No stone was left unturned; I had light tests, while probes were attached to my head to try to find out why I was having these seizure-like episodes. I had so many blood tests that I thought the nurse was a vampire in disguise and each and every time, the test came back and no problems were found.

I knew deep down it wasn't laziness, because I am what people called "driven". I became paranoid that people thought I was swinging the lead, but I wasn't. Something was wrong, but what it was, no one seemed to know. I admitted to the doctor that I was depressed but who the hell wouldn't have been? I had been an athlete but now I was turning into a couch potato and at times when I was on my own, I really did question if what I was experiencing was real.

Months went by of what me and Jo termed as "boom or bust". Some days I would feel fine and on those days, I would graft as hard as I could to try to cram everything in. It was an anxious time. I didn't know what was happening to me. Was it psychological? Or had the doctors missed something? All I knew was that it was slowly driving me mad with frustration.

It was later that year that the specialist voiced his diagnosis. "It appears that you have chronic fatigue," he said as he studied his notes. It hit me like a sledgehammer. I had heard of it before and dismissed it as "yuppie flu" and thought it only happened to other people. My next question was: "Okay, how do I get rid of it?" He replied that it would take time and I would have to accept that the road to recovery could take a long time and I wouldn't get well overnight. There was no quick fix and it was about graded living, which meant slowly trying to rebuild my life and accepting that there would be highs and lows and if I tried too hard, too fast, it would impair my recovery.

It was difficult to digest his words, but I internalised that I had lived my life on the run, always trying to play catch-up and never taking into account that I was human and needed to recover from the trauma that my body had been through.

I felt emotional. In my heart I had known that there was something wrong but had expected that they would prescribe some medication for anything they diagnosed. There was no pill, it was all about being patient and I had never been patient in my life. I would like to say that I accepted his ideas and put them into practice but anyone who is a competitor always wants to push themselves harder. It is how we differ from ordinary folk. So at first, I continued with my usual boom or bust style.

Things didn't improve for a long time and it was only when I started to approach my life by listening to my body and re-learning what I was capable of and taking time to rest not just at night but whenever I needed it. It certainly didn't happen overnight. People have always complimented me on the many adversities that I have overcome, but they haven't been with me when the blackness of despondency has descended amid times when I have felt like giving up, moments when I broke down emotionally and really questioned if I would be ever able to compete again.

Ironically for the first time in my life I learnt to congratulate myself on small achievements and not to focus on competing but to look at taking little steps and to expect that from time to time, that I would have days that were tougher than others.

I made up my mind to do some research on the illness as the consultant had told me everybody was different and some people had it more acute than others. It was both informative and frightening to read other people's experiences. The impact of chronic fatigue on the lives of some of the sufferers was so debilitating that people spent many months and in some cases years in their beds. It made me realise that although what had happened to me was causing me difficulties, on the grand scale of things, it melted into insignificance against the acute cases of these unfortunate and often maligned people.

I won't say that I approached life from then on with a positive approach. I had doubts, but I tried to focus on the positives that I wasn't so severely affected as other people and that with time I may be able to return to something near normal life.

I started out with small graded workouts to try to gauge each day what I could accomplish. I found that I could take advantage of the massive endorphin release that I experienced through exercise, while also ensuring that my diet was clean and my blood sugar was stable. I used complex carbohydrates at each meal except my post-training meal and for that I would have a mixture of both simple and complex sugars.

I wasn't driving at this point as my concentration levels at times were affected and some days I would get on the bus and go to the gym, have a coffee and come straight back home, but I always tried to go out. I remember on one occasion I had managed about 20 minutes of low intensity training and I had started to feel ill, so I just left the gym and I slowly made my way back to the bus stop. I knew that I was staggering a little bit, but as I passed two women, who were stood, idly talking to each other, I heard one of them loudly exclaim: "Look at him, drunk at this time." I looked towards them with a mixture of anger and frustration. I wanted to go up to them and tell them to keep their fucking opinions to themselves, but I was too tired and weak to go back and argue with the women.

It took many months but slowly I progressed and as time went by, it seemed my body was recovering. I would go for days at first and then weeks without crashing, but it was always hard to accept the day when I had to just go to bed. I knew I had no choice; I had to work with it. There were still times when it seemed like I was trying to scale an avalanche. Days spent in bed on a sunny day when I could hear all the activity outside, people laughing and talking while I was confined to bed like a prisoner confined to his cell. When I had days like that they seemed to loom like a foreboding shadow over my mind. I was scared of pushing too hard at times because I instinctively knew that I would have to pay for it later.

It isn't easy gauging your life. It is like living on a knife-edge and sometimes I would fight with myself internally. Part of me wanted to keep to a steady regime, devoid of any risk, but the competitor side of me knew that I had to continue to push if I was going to get back to anywhere near my old self. I can't say that I didn't experience fear and just going out sometimes when I felt ill took all my courage, but something inside my head gave me no choice. I couldn't accept that my competition days were over and so I had to get out, had to train because this was my life and my life wasn't over.

Goodnight old friend

I WAS slowly making gains in the gym. Little by little and during one of our many conversations about bodybuilding, Mike, my old friend from the boxing gym, said he had made up his mind that he wanted to compete. I agreed to help him and drew up a three-day routine for both of us.

It was tough as hell for me, but as the months wore on I was beginning to feel like I was on a level with Mike. He had a similar mentality and hunger as me and we pushed each other on.

It was surreal at times. I couldn't believe that my body was not only adapting to the intensity of training, but also thriving. When you've been ill for so long, sometimes you look out for signs of the problems coming back to haunt you and I must confess that even though I was always trying to be positive, at times, especially when I was on my own, I lived in fear of relapsing.

It is a rare thing to train with people who are as motivated as you. Usually one person is more determined than the other. You can often see guys waiting in the gym and then getting the phone call that their training partner can't make it for whatever reason and this is especially so when it's a leg day. If you have a good workout partner though, the motivation goes through the roof; you don't want to let your partner down. You turn up for workouts with an excitement because you can see the results, not just for yourself, but your training partner too.

Months went by in a flash such was the ferocity of our training sessions. All I thought about was getting back on the stage. Everything else such as weekdays and weekends became obstacles of time that stood in front of me and making my comeback. A comeback that at times had seemed impossible.

Workout days shone like golden moments of time that represented a chance to regain and increase my muscle tissue. Mike was looking well, he was always cut and I knew it wouldn't take him more than six or eight weeks to get absolutely ripped. In the past his problem had been that he didn't eat enough food but now he had set out his goal to compete with me he was trying to stick rigidly to the diet we had made out for him.

However he was having problems swallowing all the extra food. He complained a number of times about the problem, but we both put it down to the fact that maybe his oesophagus and stomach wasn't used to all the calories that he was now trying to ingest.

By 2004, we were training up to four times a week and I knew that if I was going to compete in 2005 with Mike, I was going to have to make a major decision and that was not if, but when I would use gear again. I can't say I dreaded using it, that would be a lie, but I was in a dilemma because my health had improved so much and now I was going to risk it again. You can only progress so far without using gear especially in your late 40s, and I had worked so hard over the last year so now with slight trepidation, I felt that it was time to roll the dice once again.

I ordered my first course and then promptly had to make another call to the Needle Exchange. It felt strange to be shown into a room where two other people were sat. Their features were gaunt and their eyes looked heavy. "Heroin chic" I think they call it. I found myself taking glimpses of them in the silence of that lonely room. I could see their bloodshot eyes contrasting sharply against their anaemic faces. I could feel myself tensing as one of them got up and started to nervously pace up and down. It was a relief when the door opened and a smart, very clinical looking woman ushered me in.

The Needle Exchange is a service that provides fresh syringes and a safe place to dispose of used ones. This meant having to associate with guys who were hooked on "street" drugs. I think in some ways I deluded myself into thinking that because I used steroids, I wasn't addicted like them, but then maybe we all delude ourselves. People drink and smoke and the media have highlighted the horrors of both, but human beings seem to have this inbuilt sense of "it will never happen to me". I think I had that innate sense of self too. If someone had said to me at that time that I was addicted to gear, I would have tried to take the moral high ground and stated that steroids are not chemical addictive like hard drugs such as heroin. Looking back I needed my drugs to look the way that defined me at that time.

Having got everything I needed, I watched as the worker packed my paraphernalia into a swanky looking upmarket plastic bag. As I was leaving, I could hear staff trying to calm down the guy who had been pacing up and down. He was screaming at them and raising a scrawny fist in a threatening manner. He looked so emaciated and vulnerable as two well built workers tried to usher him outside.

I couldn't help thinking that this was once someone's baby and they probably had been filled with great hope that he would live a better life than them. I found myself feeling angry that I had to share a place like this with people like him. I know now it was totally irrational, but each and every time I had to go to that place, my heart sank.

I was excited to get home and immediately prepared a hot bath for myself. I went through my usual ritual and both the forthcoming pain and nausea that always accompanied injecting myself came to fleetingly visit. I kept myself feeling positive as I injected, telling myself that this was a necessary evil to get myself back on stage and competing.

The "juice", as steroids are sometimes called, seemed to give me the edge mentally and physically. Within a few weeks, the magic… no, I shouldn't use that word because any novice reading this will think that gear is just that. Look around the gym and you will see many types of people using steroids. Some want to use it in place of good eating and training but their results will be far short of anything created by a magician's wand. Okay, enough of the lecture and let's get on.

After about four weeks I could feel myself feeling stronger and my physique started to look that much harder. Workouts were going well with Mike, but he was still having problems digesting the amount of food he needed to eat. In fact he told me a few times he had begun choking because food had stuck in his throat. After one particularly hard leg workout we were both trying to get our breath back and we began our post-session drinks of honey, porridge and whey protein and I could see that he was struggling to take it in. Noticing that I was looking at him quizzically, in a throwaway remark, Mike said that his doctor had arranged for him to have some tests because it had gone on for so long.

It was about ten on a Monday morning that Mike phoned me to say he wouldn't be able to make training that day. The results had come back from his biopsy and he had been informed that he had cancer. I just listened as though it was a bad dream. Cancer had taken my father's life but he was in his 70s and Mike was only 42. As always he was optimistic, we talked about how he had never given up on anything and how he would come through this. When I look back, the words that I tried to give him in a futile hope of offering some comfort were so trivial, but I really didn't know what to say. I even joked and asked: "Is this just an excuse not to train with me?" He just laughed but I could sense he was scared. Everything seemed so surreal and I just didn't know what to say. We ended the call, saying that once he had beaten it, I would help him compete.

It was tough though. I felt so guilty that I was okay and able to train and he was so ill. Before his next test day, I phoned him and wished him luck. In my heart I expected him to ring back and tell me what treatment he was going on and how long it would take.

Later that day, the phone rang and Jo answered and she shouted to me that it was Mike. I cheerfully greeted him and waited for him to tell me what had happened. There was an eerie silence on the other end of the phone, the sort of silence that I heard when my dad had passed away and my brother had phoned to tell me. Instinctively I knew it was bad news, but I still couldn't believe it when he managed to get himself together and told me that the tests had revealed the cancer had spread through his lungs and even into his bones and that the consultant had told him that it was terminal.

He just delivered it matter-of-fact as though reading it off a sheet. I think he was still in shock and I was on the other end of the phone frantically searching my mind for appropriate words to say, but none came. He told me that they said because of the extent of the cancer, he had about six months left.

My thoughts again went back to my father, he had been given only six months to live and he had lasted nearly three years. I relayed this to Mike, but my words felt hollow and to be honest I don't know if they were more for my benefit than Mike's. I felt absolutely numb when I finally put the phone down. I had to train back and biceps later in the day and although I went, I just couldn't concentrate and ended up jacking after a few sets.

Jo drove me down to see Mike a week later; he seemed his old self and was laughing and joking as though nothing was wrong. He had moved back in with his mum and the only sense of reality was spread across his mum's face. She looked close to tears as we chatted and, to Mike's frustration, was trying to do everything for him. "Don't fuss mother, I'll show them out," he shouted as she jumped to her feet as we were leaving.

I chatted a lot to Mike on the phone and he was always asking how my training was going and how he was going to come down and watch me compete. I used to hesitate at first about telling him that things were going well, it didn't feel right, he had set out on this journey with me and now he was going to die and I was getting healthier, but he always wanted to know if I was on target for my comeback and unbelievably he was the one encouraging me.

I will never forget the call off his mum about two months later. She told me that he was really unwell. I could tell by her voice that sounded older than her years and was laden with emotion that she thought he hadn't got long left. The drive to Mike's mum was tough, it felt really emotional but I was determined not to show him I was upset. His brother answered the door; he looked solemn, burdened with sadness. Mike and his three brothers had always been competitive to the point that sometimes it had led to blows, but now they showed their love, their unity for someone who had been such a massive influence on their lives.

I knelt down on the floor beside him. His long hair had been cut and for the first time I saw that he looked tired and weary. He had always been a real fighter in life but now it was the closing rounds and he was looking for someone to throw the towel in. I could barely hear his voice, but amazingly when he opened his eyes and saw me, he smiled and said: "How's the training going Jim?" I grinned back at him: "Not as good as it was with my old training partner pal."

I looked around me. I could see photographs of his young sons, Nick and Joe. At times like that I questioned the wisdom of any God. Mike was one of the good guys in life, if he could help someone, he would. He had once let me stay at his place when I had split with an old girlfriend and I had nowhere to live.

This thought laid heavy in my mind. Two weeks later, the same flashed through my mind as I saw the pallbearers carry his coffin into a congested church. All I remember about the funeral was his old mum, watching as he was lowered into the ground, looking like she had aged many years and was trying to stifle back tears as a friend comforted her. Her words cut the air as people threw handfuls of dirt and said their own silent goodbyes. She looked as though she had just been thrown back into reality as she said: "So that it, it's all over then?"

It was at that moment that I knew that if my body would let me I would compete on the stage, not just for me, but for my friend Mike too. It would be my way of paying respect to one of the most decent people I had ever had the privilege to meet. I didn't go to the pub afterwards like many of the people who had attended the service. I said my goodbyes to his family and slumped in the car as Jo silently drove me home.

The comeback

IN THE days that passed, I was driven again, I attacked the workouts with renewed vigour, I was determined to compete and Mike's death had shown me that you had to take chances in life if you are to live your dream.

Throughout 2005 I took different steroids on cycles of eight weeks on, 12 weeks off, and by the end of the year I had packed on over two stones in weight. Some of this would have been fat, some water, but I was hoping most of it would be muscle memory.

My friendship with John had become very close. He would often come to the flat where I lived with Jo and we would talk non-stop about bodybuilding for hours, but sure enough, on cue and almost robotic, at precisely two-hour intervals, we would stop talking and we would rise from our seats and start to ingest our next meal.

John was also planning the same shows I was going to do, the NABBA Open UK and the NAC Open British later in the year. He was in a lot better shape than me, so I knew that our preparations would be totally different. My idea was to do a number of shows beforehand and I had a lot more body fat to lose than John, so I started my "cut" to lose body fat slowly with the help of my friend Ben as usual.

As well as dieting and cardio I used another product called ephedrine, which was a stimulant to both burn body fat and give you more focus and energy. A lot of the guys were using it, but it does have side-effects and one of them is to shrink one's genitals for a short period of time. Some were even taking it with Viagra, which meant they had a rock hard, but very short and skinny penis.

I got a phone call from one of my old mates one day and he sounded really worried. I will spare his blushes and not reveal his name. He definitely wasn't his usual confident self, in fact his voice was a mere whisper, but seemed to echo and I had to ask him to speak up. He seemed strangely harassed and after a brief chat, he explained that he was in a very precarious position.

Apparently he had taken refuge in the bathroom of his new girlfriend after they had fallen in a heap of passion and at the height of arousal for the both of them, he had looked down and found he had very little to consummate the act with. I could hardly stop myself from exploding with laughter at the mental image of this massive bodybuilder hiding away in the toilet. I teased him and asked if he was sure it wasn't always that size as it had never happened to me, but in the end, I had to put him out of his misery and after I stopped laughing long enough, I calmed him down and told him the truth. I don't think he ever saw her again and apparently that night she didn't see much of him either. Sorry pal if you are reading this, but it was funny and that's ephedrine for you, it gives you loads of energy to make love but very little to do it with!

I also got training with a young guy called Ian. He wanted to join the Navy but was motivated as hell to train. He reminded me of when I set out; skinny, motivated, but with little idea of how to train. I remember talking to him about how I was trying to get in shape to compete. It was tough without Mike around and when Ian volunteered to be my training partner, I must confess I thought in my mind that he wouldn't last more than a few sessions. I was back in to hardcore training and I was doubtful that he would be willing to take such punishment.

When he turned up the next day, I was surprised because I knew that some of the guys from the gym had been goading him about taking out life insurance because if he trained with me, he was going to die. But there he was, looking slightly nervous and dressed in what I call "fitness gear". Shorts, vest and trainers adorned his tall, skinny frame as he strode in and met me as I was wrapping bandages around my knees and adjusting the shoelaces on my steel toecap lifting boots.

The workouts were based around compound movements such as squats, dead-lifts, rows, dips, and bench presses. Squats and dead-lifts are avoided by many people because they are so tough. If you train hard enough you can't help but scream, such is the pain. You can hardly breathe and you can always tell someone who does "deads" on a regular basis as their shins are scraped and their thighs chaffed.

We were training quads and I was preparing to go to war on the free squat and there was no room for training partners who wanted to go AWOL, but I needn't have feared. Ian was one determined guy. He would turn red, then white and finally green before making a mad dash for the toilet to be sick and every workout I thought that would be it, he wouldn't turn up again, but he did.

He was getting stronger and it was having a positive effect on my training too. His infectious determination forced me to dig deeper and deeper. I had created a monster, and at times it was me hanging on. The chronic fatigue still reared its ugly head and the intensive training left me exhausted and some days I would have to go to bed at 6pm because I was so shattered. I had doubts, real fears at times that the journey would end abruptly, with more chance of me being hospitalised than actually competing on stage, but there was little I could do but to hang on to the express train that our workout regime had become.

I was still getting the odd abscess or I would suddenly get vertigo. I would have to scrape myself off the floor sometimes and then on shaky legs sit or lie down. As for positive mental attitude, at times I totally ran out of it and sometimes it felt easier to admit defeat. These were days when it seemed easier to raise the white flag and I often had doubts that my health was up to the massive stress that competing was placing on my body, but something deep inside me kept me going.

I never allowed myself to think ahead more than the next workout. Competing seemed like a promised land that maybe I would never reach. I had concerns right up to the first competition if my body would hold out, but out of sheer dedication, well if I'm honest, it was at times more like pure desperation, it did.

My friend Mike was never far away from my mind and sometimes when I felt like giving in, I would remember how much he had longed to compete and that became my driving force too. I figured the only way I wouldn't compete was if I collapsed completely. I felt that I owed it to Mike's memory to give my all, but I wasn't deluding myself either, I knew that despite all the training that I had managed to get in, I still wasn't the same athlete that I had been before my accident.

I started dieting in May. Despite everything it was a slow process, my last show had been in 1999 and now it was six years later and my body was responding differently to the diet than it had done before. As the body fat came off, my trainer Ben took a look at me and his honest appraisal was that I had lost a fair amount of muscle tissue over the last few years. I knew that I still had to get leaner, but I decided to have a go at the famous Wigan show in September. It is one of the few all-round shows that looks to entertain the crowd with cabaret and karaoke.

The day of the competition came and as I queued with the other competitors, it felt like my first show again and I could feel my adrenaline pumping hard. It was good to see my old mate Kevin from the Bodyzone gym had joined the line to sign in. He looked huge, I knew that he had competed and done well in some international shows. It was good to catch up and it helped settle my nerves.

The room was rocking as the MC strutted his stuff on stage and bellowed out a Robbie Williams number. It was a fantastic atmosphere as the crowd really got into party mode and as I sat there with my friends, I tried to relax. The first class on stage came out, four juniors, well three juniors and one lad who looked huge and muscular far beyond his years. As someone shouted out, he did indeed look to have muscle even in his spit.

As the classes came out I began to feel edgy, I knew that I wasn't in top shape yet and I just didn't want to show myself up. The call eventually came for the master class to go backstage. Jo got up first and I think she was as nervous as I was. The changing room was small and some of the guys were already there. I tried to avoid any eye contact as we squeezed in among the other guys and Jo started to apply my tan.

It seemed to take ages and the old psychological feeling came to visit me. One of my friends who is a top heavyweight told me once that at times even he felt small compared to others and here in the testosterone-filled air backstage I felt like a little skinny kid again.

In one of the mirrors I tried out some poses and my heart felt like it was going to make a guest appearance as it threatened to leap out of my chest. I was relieved when we got the go-ahead to take the stage. My mouth felt dry as I summoned up the cheesy grin and flared my back wide and hit my quads hard. I had forgotten how hot the stage lights were and as I wiped the trickle of sweat that mingled with my false tan, I could hear my mates and Jo shouting for me and the stage nerves started to ebb as the roar of the crowd flowed through my veins.

The cobwebs were falling away and I could feel a smile that wasn't forced eclipsing my whole face as I felt the overwhelming charge of adrenaline and serotonin. I was back, maybe not at my best, but in the dark times when I had been so ill I could barely stand up, this moment had seemed a faraway dream.

I felt at home as I was called out in the first round. It was music to my ears to hear the grunts of the other bodybuilders forcing out their poses. I was giving everything; all the thoughts of trying to pace myself had long since become submerged in a frenzy of energy I no longer thought I possessed.

I honestly can't recall much detail of the show, just the incredible atmosphere. It seemed to be over in a heartbeat, time seemed to be fast forwarding like a video machine, until suddenly it was all over and the MC was asking us to go to the back of the stage to await our placing. I tried to keep my physique tensed, but suddenly fatigued floated in, enveloping me in its grip, and I could feel my body sliding into a half-baked attempt to keep "tight". I couldn't have given a damn where I had finished; I was just relieved that I made it through the show in one piece.

The medals were given out and one by one, guys stepped forward, leaving just three competitors and to my surprise, I was one of them. I had a mass monster to my left, he was big but lacked conditioning, and the other guy who looked of a similar stature to me, except for his quads which lacked the mass of mine.

His physique definitely had that ripped look though and on that day the judges went for condition. It was no surprise that he took the title, but I was shocked to be awarded second place and I also walked off with the most muscular prize too. As I drifted back to my friends, I found myself staring at the bronze statue and the most muscular medal and thinking: "Any moment now I'll wake up!"

The Blackpool show a week later was fun too, well both fun and extremely weird. I have never been one of the guys who attracts groupies but as I was sat there with Jo, this girl got talking to us as if Jo didn't exist. She went into this dialogue about being an expert in applying tan and how she had helped loads of top bodybuilders backstage. She then offered out of total altruistic madness to tan me up. I told her in no uncertain terms that Jo would be coming backstage with me, but to both our amazements, she didn't take the hint and continued to offer her professional touch. I don't know what planet or drugs she was on, but Jo and I took the chance while she was diverted by an announcement from the MC to make our escape. We stealthily crept away and made it to the "sanity", well sanctuary, of the backstage area.

I was just starting to relax and had even started to laugh with Jo about the incident when out of the corner of my eye, like the shark from *Jaws*, this woman made her entrance. It was terrifying. Her smile shot straight at me and it was at this stage I thought drastic action was needed so I dragged my bag and Jo off to the nearest place of safety. We ended up locking ourselves into the cramped disabled changing rooms and amid much laughter from us both, Jo started to apply the Dream Tan, which is just a one-coat tan that is supposed to be easily removable but stains just about everything you touch. I remember that because I playfully tapped Jo's behind when she had finished tanning me and it left a brown hand imprint on her white trousers. I didn't tell her about it until after the show though!

When we were called on stage we had to walk through the audience to get there and suddenly I felt a sharp pain that I hadn't had in years. It wasn't sciatica; my serial stalker had seated herself with a group of women and pinched my arse. It had been so long since a woman had done that

I was that startled I gasped out aloud. To be honest, part of me felt elated, until I saw Jo's eyes, she was definitely not amused. I felt more like a stripper than a bodybuilder, scantily clad in posing trunks among a sea of spectators, but I was slightly upset that no women bothered to tip me by putting money down my briefs.

There were five guys in my class, including Dave, who had beat me in Wigan. He was looking even sharper now and it was no surprise that despite my best efforts, he took first place again.

I had done no carb loading. For me this was just another show to sharpen up with and to break the monotony of training and I was happy with second place, but ended up being talked into doing a height class that was to take place later in the day. It was my treat day and I sat with Jo munching on cheese and pickle sandwiches and even a muffin washed down with a diet coke. I was happy to watch other competitors and when the two height categories were called backstage, there was my nemesis Dave, getting ready again.

I smiled to myself and cast an eye around the room. Besides Dave there were another three competitors in my class. I felt really chilled out as Jo applied the tan and yes I was still on my guard and I did keep an eye out in case the tanning lady returned. I felt good as I pumped up, the fast-acting carbs that I had ingested were obviously working and I could feel the blood pumping hard through my veins. I had a quick look in the mirror just before we were called on and I could see that my physique was improving in both hardness and cut.

The first call-out brought me and Dave, with a guy who had a good chest, back and delts but lacked quad development, into the firing line. I just made sure that I hit every pose hard, trying to squeeze each muscle as the MC shouted them out. I felt good and my energy levels gave me the push to ensure that I was next to Dave in the pose-down. Where he went I went, when he hit a pose, I made sure I hit one harder.

The MC's voice trailed over the rock music to tell us to take our place at the back of the stage, but the guys kept on posing. No one seemed to want to stop as the crowd continued to roar their approval and urge us on! Reluctantly I filed into line and was shaking hands with the guys as the placings were announced. It came down to me and Dave again, but as we stood flexing our physiques in preparation of the judge's decision, there seemed to be much debating going on.

Now most people will think that this can't happen, but it did and it just goes to prove how carbing up is such a finite art. In the morning I had lost to Dave but now, a few hours later, I got the verdict over him. Dave took it in good spirit and asked me what I had done in the interlude between the two competitions. I smiled and told him it was a carbing up technique that I was experimenting with. I didn't have the heart to tell him that he had got beaten by an entrée of cheese and pickle butties, finished off by a chocolate chip muffin and diet coke!

It was back to the dreaded cardio the next day and the next few weeks were going to be tough; I still had more body fat to lose and about four weeks to do it in. I met up with Ben again and we discussed going as low as 100 carbohydrates a day with just one re-feed day, where I would take my carbohydrates up to 500. To anyone who doesn't know what that feels like, you need around 100 carbs for brain function, so the closest description I can think of to tell you how I felt at this stage is you know those zombie movies, well I could have been definitely typecast as one of the zombies and I probably wouldn't have needed any make-up.

Now it was getting hard. Most days I felt like I was walking on sand. I wasn't as strong as I had previously been, three years of fighting for my health had taken its toll, but

I was determined to see it through. When you're dieting and training so hard the days go slowly; non-competitors don't understand when they say: "Oh you've only got a few weeks before the show!" Two weeks means two all-out sessions of each muscle group, numerous amounts of cardio and trying to survive on small amounts of food. You don't live from day to day, you digest one small meal and then think about the next helping that is two hours away. Many times I have chased the last few grains of rice around a plate because at that moment in time they were mine and every grain counted.

The week before the first championship I met up with Ben. I felt like death and wearily stripped down so he could have a look at me. I struggled to pull off a few mandatory poses and then I heard the words that I had wanted to hear for so many weeks: "You're spot on Jim!"

I had done it, it had been one of the toughest journeys of my life but I had finally got into the condition that all bodybuilders aspire to. Your skin is so transparent that every muscle can be clearly defined. It is strange how little things can fill you with adrenaline isn't it? For weeks I had staggered through everything, never giving an inch but totally exhausted, and now I felt exhilarated. I knew that I was about a stone down from the last time I competed but I didn't care. I was going to compete next week and now it was time to fine-tune everything with carbing up and water manipulation.

Driving loco in Dudley

THE DAY of the NABBA UK in Dudley arrived; John had assured me that he would drive as Jo had other commitments. He arrived early and after saying goodbye to Jo, we went down to the car he had just bought. I was feeling totally relaxed and happy to let John drive, but I noticed that he seemed a little tense. I stupidly put that down to pre-competition nerves.

It was when we reached the motorway, about a mile from my home, that I became aware we were undertaking vehicles and John was speeding right up to the back of cars, before hitting the brakes hard. I had settled back into passenger mode as I usually did when driving to a show but now I was alert. I wasn't thinking about the show, I was now thinking about survival.

It transpired that John had only passed his test a couple of days before and this was his first time on a motorway. I wouldn't call it driving really, I would call it dodgems. My doubts about his driving ability were reinforced when he put the wipers on because it was raining and no water came out and the wipers went to and fro, scraping all sorts of dirt across the windscreen, until we couldn't see properly and had to get on the hard shoulder to wipe it off.

In the end I managed to eventually persuade him to pull into a motorway services and by this time, I needed the toilet badly. I don't know if it was through the water loading or just that my nerves were shredded. I guess we had gone about 40 miles, but it did seem longer, mainly as I felt my life had flashed before my eyes on several occasions.

I don't know if it was through fear, the fact that I had dieted for so long or that we went through some kind of time warp, but after watching John drive so erratically, I had lost track of where we should get off the motorway and when I finally did get him to pull in, we weren't in Dudley, we were in South Wales. I couldn't believe it. I did a quick look to the heavens to see if there was a flying saucer overhead, but nope, there were no signs of any aliens and we hadn't been abducted. We had missed the junction where we should have come off, not just by a few miles, but around 50.

We were in the middle of nowhere and all I could think was don't panic, stress holds water, so I talked John into letting me drive for a while meaning he could rest and take in some food. We had done several miles and I was following the signs for Dudley. We had set out in good time but now our detour meant that we had very little room for error. I could hear John chomping away on some food and the radio was churning out some road music. It had been so long since I had driven because of being ill and I felt unbelievably chilled as we both relaxed in the thought we were now heading the right way.

As we turned off the motorway, John pointed out the signs indicating Dudley and then as if the thought had just hit him he exclaimed: "Hey Jim how come Jo always drives? You're a good driver pal." I thought about it for a while. I hadn't been able to drive for so long because of the black-outs and to be honest I had lost confidence, but being at the wheel again felt so natural. "It's because I had some kind of seizures pal," I replied eventually, not thinking too much about what I was saying.

John's face was a picture as he choked and spewed his food out. "Fuck me pal, you could have told me that before you started driving!" he eventually blurted out.

I smiled and thought how this trip had been so eventful, but unbelievably, we were turning in to the venue and at that very moment they were just opening the doors for the crowd to go in. We waved to people we knew and then parked up and strolled over to the back of the queue. John said we looked real cool, like we had planned to arrive at the last moment.

We both booked in and I don't know why but I lost all track of time again. I was laughing and joking with some friends and telling them the story of how we ended up in South Wales when John came running back to me. It seemed my category was first on and all the other guys were backstage. We both dashed there and all the guys had their tan on and were pumping up. I stripped, got my posing pouch on and John and another friend started tanning me up with Dream Tan. We had about half of it on when the MC came back and informed us that there was no time left and they wanted us on stage, but we didn't listen. It was all hands to the pump and even a girl from another group joined in with the new game of "painting Jim by numbers".

I got to the back of the stage just as they were going on and as I went on, I was still busily patting my tan down and hoping it covered everything. I had no time to pump up and felt flat as a pancake. I was breathing hard as I joined the other guys on stage and by now I was in a state of panic, ruing the amateurish mistakes that I had made. All the preparation that I done; now it all felt wasted and I felt like kicking myself as I got into competition mode and gave the crowd the usual "cheesy, confident grin".

There were only four people in my group. I was so knackered through running around like a madman backstage but as soon as I heard the first mandatory pose called out, I bit my lip and ground my quads into the floor and hit the pose like my life depended on it. They compared us all as part of a group so there was no break in proceedings. I was giving it my all and could feel the blood exploding into my veins as I squeezed my muscles into the appropriate poses. I know it was psychological, but I still didn't feel like I had got a proper pump and as soon as we were taken off to come back for our own individual rounds, I ran off to ingest the chocolate I had in my bag, to try to get some simple sugars into my body and help with pumping up.

The other guys were doing some simple exercises as the first guy was called back on stage. I was like a hamster on speed as I frantically did push-ups, dips, anything to try to feel a pump, but I honestly had written off my chances and in my mind was putting it down to experience and vowing that it wouldn't happen again as my name was called to do my individual posing.

I was the last one on and the crowds were appreciative and knowledgeable as they roared their approval as I exploded through my routine to the theme from *Pulp Fiction*. It all happened so quickly after that. We went to the back of the stage, they announced fourth, I went to go forward, but it wasn't me. They announced third and it was the guy to my right. I stood there with the last competitor; it had come down to him and me. I nervously looked at him, he looked heavier and in as good shape as me. I was happy to take second, but at that moment the MC shouted out my name as the NABBA UK Masters champion. It was one of those moments that take an age for you to realise it isn't a dream and what you are experiencing is actually real.

I went backstage to where John was pumping up. I was in a trance and just sat on the floor near him, putting my trophy in my bag and got some chicken out and started munching. John, fearing that all the problems we encountered had jeopardised my chances, said: "Sorry mate, it's my fault we were late." I couldn't answer as I was munching food and I wasn't really taking in what he had said and then I heard him say: "How did you go on?"

"I won pal," was all I could muster. He was doing some side lateral raises at the time and stopped dead in his tracks as he had mistaken my dazed state as me being grumpy about losing. He seemed to take time to digest what I had said and then shouted in a voice that sounded both incredulous and happy. "You won it?" I smiled. "Yep," I replied, and then it hit me.

Okay it wasn't one of the major trophies, but with all of the health problems that I had, it was nothing short of a miracle. I had to take myself away for a few moments as I could feel my emotions finally overcoming me and I knew my pal was going on stage in a few minutes and I had to help him get ready.

There were only a few guys in John's class and the guy who was his main rival was a mass monster. John had the edge in definition and quality, but this guy was huge and eventually the judges decided that on this day, they would go for bulk over condition. I don't think John was too upset as his main show would be the NAC in a week's time. He was even smiling and laughing with me as we got into his car and suddenly the prospect of driving hundreds of miles back home in the dark with a guy who had only just passed his test loomed heavily on my mind. To my amazement though, the journey home, apart from losing our way a few times, was a lot less traumatic. John put it down to the fact that his driving had improved. I just thought: "No, it's because there are fewer cars to hit at this time of night!"

Showdown at the NAC

IT WAS back to the gym the following day. John and I used to meet up and do the dreaded cardio together. I think it was because we were so cognitively challenged by the lack of food that we were on the same wavelength and understood how each other felt. The rest of the gym seemed to be filled with alien species. They smiled, chatted and laughed their way through their workouts but we seldom smiled, grunted and made little conversation. We would be on the bikes for over an hour and it was comforting to know that John was going through the same misery as I was.

Our communication skills had long since deserted us. We would grunt out a sentence now and again to each other, incoherent to the rest of humanity, but making total sense to us. People would interrupt now and again and hit us both with long drawn-out sentences and we would look at each other while pedalling away and wish the other one would take the lead and answer, but often we would just look at the person blankly. We were in a world only other bodybuilders who are so depleted would know.

The day of the NAC show at Middleton arrived. It started at four o'clock and most of the gym was coming down to watch John and I compete. It was only a few miles from where I lived, so I spent the early morning trying to relax as once again I had spent the whole night going to the toilet.

We queued outside and it was nice to see so many familiar faces such as Kris who ran the gym for Joe. We huddled around waiting for the doors to open and believe me when you are down to five per cent body fat you are never warm, even on a sunny day, and this was a dark evening in November.

When we got in we found the signing-in room and got our numbers. There were only three people in my class and the same number in John's. With so many people about and so much time to fill, John and I sought refuge and found the most ideal place. We reckoned the disabled toilets would give us some respite from all the commotion going on outside. We both lay on the floor and started munching on our next meal but we had forgotten one thing; to tell our partners where we were hiding and unknown to us they had spent ages going around the venue before they got told by one of our friends that we were in the disabled toilets. When John heard the door being rattled he thought it was unwelcome guests and began to make "farting" noises to get them to go away. Eventually after much reluctance on our part, we answered the door to see Jo and Christina, their disapproving faces looking at us eating our food in a smelly toilet.

I was first on and John came backstage with Jo and helped me tan up. One of the people who had helped me over the years came backstage to see me just before I started to pump up and secretly slipped this tablet in my hand and told me it would bring out my vascularity. In other words it would make my veins stand out. I looked closely at the tablet. I had seen it before and then it hit me what this was.

He had given me Viagra. Now to me this wasn't a good idea, particularly with the fact that I was going to be out on stage with over 500 people watching me, while I was wearing nothing more than a tiny pair of posing trunks.

I told him there was no chance and we argued. He said it wouldn't affect me as Viagra only worked when you are in the mood. After a heated discussion and the fact he had always given me good advice, I swallowed the tablet but my head said: "I hope he is bloody right." I ate my chocolate, swallowed my red wine, mixed with glycerine and creatine to make me look even more vascular and also to help with the pump. After five minutes I was warm, very warm. I was also nervous, not about losing but getting a full-blown erection on the stage and inadvertently showing the crowd that some parts of me weren't in symmetry.

The other two guys who were competing lined up behind me. They both looked good but had completely different physiques. One guy was tall and he had a top-heavy physique and needed more work on his quads; the other guy was from a gym in Middleton and had lots of support in the audience. He was shorter but had an all-round good physique and although he was in condition, he wasn't ripped.

We got called on stage and we were told to go straight into free posing to warm the crowd up. I could hear my friends going wild in the crowd but the thought of them seeing more of me than they bargained for weighed heavy on my mind. I nervously went through each pose thinking of the least sexual thing I could. At one stage I thought of a famous lady Conservative and instantly internalised on how much therapy I would need if I got aroused visualising her.

The two other lads were of a good standard and they worked us hard under the hot lights, but for the first time since I had come back I felt the adrenaline pumping, I was flowing easily through each pose and I didn't need to put on a false grin. In fact, I was smiling from ear to ear; it just felt fantastic to be in such good form on the NAC British stage in front of my family and friends.

No one gave an inch; it was warfare out there, survival of the fittest. The other guys followed me around the stage and to the roar of the crowd; they smashed out one dynamic pose after another. I think we must have spent a good few minutes warming up the crowd until the music stopped and we were brought in line.

The first call was to turn to our right for a side profile so the judges could view each contestant from every angle. It seemed an age that they kept us there and then I heard laughter from the crowd, but I held my position hard and then I realised what had happened. The bald-headed guy had turned completely the opposite way and amid the confusion me and the smaller guy turned back around thinking we had made the mistake. After much chaos and laughter from the audience, we eventually got in line. I don't know if it's because of the low carbs or some bodybuilders just have no sense of direction, but it's not unusual to see this. There may have been only three of us but they worked us hard by making us interchange position and calling out more comparisons.

The Viagra that I had taken certainly made me look vascular, and thankfully there were no signs of my little friend making a guest appearance. Finally though, the MC amid screams and whistles from the crowd shouted: "Pose-down." And we all stepped out together, mirroring each other's poses and trying desperately to out-muscle each other. The music stopped after about a minute and to be honest I was thankful it had as I shook hands with my fellow competitors and wearily made my way to the back of the stage.

The results were announced and the guy with the bald head was given third place, the shorter guy with the muscular but less cut physique was called second and to my own disbelief and ears, the MC turned to the crowd and said: "A big hand please for your NAC British Masters champion, Jim Moore!"

It felt almost surreal as I stood there with my friends and family screaming out their approval. It felt as though everything was in slow motion as the cup was brought to me. I had to feel if it was real and not just one of the many dreams about this moment that I had when I was ill. I looked at the person handing me the coveted trophy; my trainer, Ben. He had been asked to hand out the cups and hadn't told me. He shook my hand and I looked down to see my Jo and then some other familiar faces looking up at me through the haze of the stark stage lights. They were going berserk and everyone seemed in a frenzy of excitement, so much so that I could barely hear the photographer shout out the poses. I was on auto pilot by now, floating on a cloud, basking in the stage light and I didn't want the moment to end. It was only when the MC's voice filtered through that I had qualified to go to the Universe championships in Aachen that I realised just what I had done.

People see competitors at sporting venues, they see them at one specific moment fulfilling their dream, but they don't see them when they are doing hours of inhuman training or in the dark days when they have faced adversity in the form of injury and illness and had to fight through the physical and psychological barriers to get to the competition. As the song says, "my one moment in time had arrived", and as the cheers of the crowd subsided and I reluctantly left the stage, Jo was waiting.

I didn't have to tell her that now the emotional rollercoaster that I had been on had finally surfaced because she could see it in my eyes. I had spent so long fighting to overcome my health problems that I had never allowed myself to feel any self-pity. I had trained and fed myself like a machine, not ever allowing myself to feel human, because I was afraid that if I let any feelings in, I would have weakened and maybe I would have raised the white flag.

It was only now in Jo's loving embrace that the iron shutters I had erected between me and the world melted in an avalanche of feelings that left me laughing and crying uncontrollably. It was several minutes before I could pull myself together and we both walked back slowly into the crowded arena to our family and friends. By then my tears had been replaced by sheer pleasure. I was walking on air, the tiredness that I had felt while on stage had gone and now I made my way through cheers and back-slaps from everyone.

Amid much banter and laughter I could hear John's class being announced and then there was a hushed silence as we all sank back into our chairs and got into spectator mode again. We shouted and cheered as the guys from class three swept on to the stage, straight into free posing and building the crowd up into a wild frenzy of noise.

John was like a ballerina when he posed. He would build the routine so it flowed, emphasising each dynamic pose for just long enough, before effortlessly contorting his body into another statuesque representation of muscularity. He looked confident but the opposition at this level was tough and while he was in his usual sliced and diced condition, there were two guys who had slightly denser muscle but who were not as defined. I could see when the results were announced that he wasn't happy, he had finished third, but had still qualified for the Universe.

Germany here we come

THE GUYS from the gym were ecstatic and Joe the owner was over the moon that his gym had two representatives in such an elite competition. I didn't want the night to end, I had qualified for the Universe, the scrawny kid who once had looked in awe at the physiques of Schwarzenegger, Columbo and Zane was now going to follow in their footsteps. Surprisingly, after many hours feasting in the kitchen, I actually slept well.

The Universe was only one week away. I was 12 and a half stone and the reality was that through my forced absence from the sport I was about 14lbs lighter, so my chances of winning were non-existent. I know people might think it was a defeatist notion but it wasn't, it was an honest appraisal by not just me but my trainer Ben.

I mulled over if it was going to be worth making the trip to Germany. The hotel had been paid for but the flights were expensive and in some ways it seemed a futile journey to be an also-ran. Part of me thought maybe I should now concentrate on returning to off-season training and try to get back the muscle tissue that I had lost.

I ended up changing my mind a number of times before finally agreeing to go. I knew in my heart that no matter what the result, I was going to do my best and that this experience would only help me, but mostly I was proud to be invited. It all seemed crazily unreal that after so much adversity I was going to set foot on one of the biggest bodybuilding stages in the world.

Joe arranged for the papers to come down and take pictures of us. It was great publicity for him and they had me and John performing numerous poses for pictures in our local paper and in the interview, it came out that I had been out of the game for six years through illness. The paper did a full page spread and it was nice to see bodybuilding being shown in such a positive light.

After it was printed, other papers reported it and then it came to the attention of a number of magazines. It was amazing to have such publicity and quite a surprise that the magazines were so interested in me and the bonus was they were actually going to pay me for it. I spent days in deep contemplation about which magazine had the integrity to write the article in the most favourable way. I had my scruples; I wasn't a man who could be bought easily. I would demand that they made a true representation that would take the message to the people that bodybuilding was a good sport to become involved with.

Unfortunately though, *Bella* magazine realised that my integrity cost about £450 and at that price they could write what they wanted.

I didn't sleep the night before. I knew we had to be at the airport at six o'clock in the morning and John and Christine were arriving at three o'clock. I felt half dead when I climbed into the taxi and we arrived at Manchester Airport and met up with some of the other guys competing.

You won't believe it and maybe I was experiencing some kind of delusional episode, but there were clowns at the airport. No, I am not having a go at the checking-in staff at the airport. There were several clowns doing magic tricks at 5am. I think that they were part of a group with children with disabilities. It was a strange experience to see clowns getting on the same flight as us, but thankfully none of them were actually flying the plane.

I am nervous about flying, but the way the seating worked out was that Christina was near the window, John in the middle and me next to him. Jo was sat across the aisle from me. I think our flight had to be one of the most bumpy journeys I have ever made and I soon found out John didn't like flying either. It didn't take me long to realise it either. At the take-off I had just shut my eyes and started trying to relax when he grabbed my wrist and growled: "I don't like the take-off." I thought: "Fuck me pal, the fact my wrist is turning blue sort of tells me that."

It was hectic when we arrived. We had to get a connecting train to Cologne and we had little time to get there. We had to run along the long connecting corridors that had those moving pathways that resemble horizontal escalators, but seem to move at a snail's pace, especially when you are in a hurry. After our unscheduled cardio we finally and breathlessly reached the train, and by now I was very excited, my dream was actually happening. The journey by train was relaxing and when we reached Cologne, I was feeling tired, but chilled.

It wasn't until we went to collect out luggage off the train that I realised that there was a problem. It wasn't on there. I was fuming and demanded they find out where it was, but even after numerous phone calls by one of the staff it seemed our cases couldn't be found. Eventually after about an hour, a uniformed member of staff came out of the office to where we were sat and casually told us that our bags were still at the airport but they would be sent on to us. Now to most people that would be okay, but apart from having all my competition gear in them, there were somewhat dubious substances in them too. I was totally pissed, but decided that if they saw me getting stressed they may suspect something, so I smiled and thanked them and turned around thinking: "I've got to relax, I've got a show tomorrow."

The girls negotiated a price for the taxi to take us to our hotel in Aachen. I was highly impressed that they got the price down so much and I took my place in the front with the driver while Jo, John and Christina sat in the back. I closed my eyes and relaxed but soon into the trip I realised we had the taxi driver from hell, either that or the girls had got such a low price that the guy felt depressed and was trying to commit suicide.

He was swerving in and out of traffic and even John's driving when he had taken me to South Wales had been better. I don't know what the guy was on but the journey was far from relaxing, although John had fallen asleep or maybe he had just passed out through fright. I must admit that I heaved a massive sigh of relief as the taxi finally came to rest outside our hotel. I had never been so grateful to put my feet on terra firma. Either the guy was a former Grand Prix driver or he didn't have a licence at all. I had been feeling tired as we boarded the taxi but now I was in open-eyed, full alert mode as I staggered towards the entrance to the hotel.

The sight that met me did little to make me feel any easier. The reception was wall to wall with people of all different nationalities and we struggled to squeeze through the hordes of people aimlessly standing around.

I finally found Bernie, the over-50s champion, and he and some of the other guys helped us sign in. I could sense the anxiety in a few of the guys and thought that it mirrored my own trepidation. I spent some time just chatting and trying to look as relaxed as possible, but the atmosphere inside the cramped area of the hotel was highly charged with a mixture of testosterone, adrenaline and fear. I found out that the some of the other athletes from the other teams had also had their luggage mislaid like ours and apparently they were in precisely the same predicament that I was.

It was a nervous few hours that I waited with them in the hotel to see if we were competing the next day or we would be getting a guided tour of the local police station. In the end though, I had to leave them to venture out into the dusky streets of Aachen on a scouting expedition for some decent water. Finding a low sodium variety in a country where the traffic flows the opposite way isn't good for a bodybuilder who is tired and doesn't have a clue of the language.

Jo walked what seemed miles with me to find some and to be honest I was totally out on my feet. I needed sleep, not a sight-seeing expedition through Aachen. My mind couldn't adjust to the fact that traffic was flowing the opposite way and if it hadn't been for Jo, I would have spent my night either in a hospital after being hit by a car or in the local nick for performing neo-Nazi salutes at the drivers who seemed to be constantly hooting me.

At about 9.30pm I was sat in my room anxiously awaiting the arrival of our cases when all of a sudden I heard the distinctive wailing of police sirens shrieking to a halt, closely followed by the receptionist phoning me to say that my luggage had arrived. I looked at Jo and all I could think was: "Fuck!" I got myself together and went downstairs to see not the police, but an elderly, harassed-looking taxi driver struggling with a number of suitcases and I could see that ours were there. As I looked around the room I could sense the guys heaving a sigh of relief. They were going to be competitive bodybuilders representing their countries, not jailbirds requiring their national ambassador.

It seemed the police cars had stopped across the road and they were sorting out a bar fight and the call to the room had been a mere coincidence. I couldn't help but smile as I went back up to the room and I just collapsed next to Jo and told her what had happened. I felt absolutely knackered and just fell on to the bed. I thought that I could sleep on a washing line, I was that drowsy. I got the cushions in place to elevate my feet because I was paranoid that the flight over had made me puff up with water.

After leaning over and kissing Jo I thought: "Right, sleep here we come." Yeah right! It doesn't matter how tired I am, the night before a competition I never sleep. I could hear Jo softly snoozing and then I had to take the first of many trips to the toilet. I think the last time I looked at the clock, it was 4am and I still there, eyes closed, thinking that if I didn't open my eyes, I might just sleep. I must have dropped off though because the alarm went at 6.30am. As I stumbled to my feet to make a coffee for me and Jo, I I felt like I could kip for England but I had to be up and get ready for the biggest show of my life.

I could barely keep my eyes open as we applied more tan before going down for breakfast. The whole place was buzzing with the tones of different languages. It was surreal watching all these people, adorned in various brands of false tan meticulously picking out their favourite pre-competition breakfasts. Some had mounds of toast and jam on their plates, others had big pieces of steak, but when I eventually found John and Christina, he had exactly the same as me: seven boiled eggs to be precise.

Conversation wasn't exactly flowing. I could see that this wasn't exactly the girls' idea of a trip abroad and at that time in the morning, I think they had turned their hearing off as John and I talked about the competition. Eugene came up to our table and told us that the first coach would be there about 8am and for me to get on as it was only meant for the senior over 40s and 50s competitors. When it did arrive though, a rush of people packed into it. All I could think was that if that lot were over 40 they must either have had a company that supplied Botox as a sponsor or they had lived a very stress-free life.

It was standing room only as me and Jo managed to squeeze into the coach. If you were claustrophobic you would have been in trouble. Whatever direction the venue was it must have been close and thankfully for the sardine-packed competitors, we were soon released and what lay before me took my breath away.

I have seen many beautiful arenas such as Wembley, but the Exhibition Hall in Aachen surpassed everything I had ever seen. The building overshadowed all in its wake. It was aesthetically stunning. Its exterior had massive panes of glass and you could see people inside the building resembling little ants going about their work. The early-morning winter sun gleamed off the glass and dazzled all who were near.

There seemed to be literally hundreds of people milling around and even when the doors were finally opened to the masses, you could feel the surge of the crowd clambering to get in first. They couldn't have all been competing, but they seemed to be determined to get whereever they were going. I began to feel edgy. The crowds seemed endless but it seemed people were being turned away and they were only letting the senior competitors sign in. The Germans are renowned for efficiency and on this occasion, despite the hordes of people, they certainly lived up to their reputation. I was processed and given my number within minutes.

Eugene led us to a massive changing room, everything was covered in thick see-through plastic strips of about ten feet wide and they ran from floor to ceiling. Even the loo seats had covered tops; this was all to try to prevent staining from competitors using Dream Tan. As I found a place to put down my stuff, I saw John coming into the room with Christina and it was good to see them in a room full of strangers. All around us, men and women were in various stages of undress. There was no separation of sexes and I think both Jo and Christina got more than an eyeful.

I know there were some beautiful fitness women in there too and I am sure that on any other occasion I would have been able to tell you in graphic detail what they looked like, but this was before a show and all I knew was that I felt nervous as I tried to relax among the many athletes who shared our room.

I could see Bernie across the room. He had his friend Ian with him and they were going through the ritual of pumping up. His face looked relaxed but I am sure that internally he must have been feeling nervous, because he was one of the top 50-year-old bodybuilders of his era and he had a good chance of taking the title.

My category was the second on but I knew there were 15 guys in Bernie's line-up so we had some time. I was sat there with my mouthful of the special flapjacks that Jo had made for me to pump up with.

John and Jo were helping me to tan up and then I noticed her; well I say her, she was huge, massively muscled and cut to hell. All the guys were looking at her and I am sure many of us were sharing the same thought that we were glad that she wasn't in their class.

There was another lady who really looked masculine; her body looked chiselled, she had bad acne, but it was mostly evident in her face. You could see the signs of stubble and her jaw line looked thick and heavy. Ironically she had a very feminine posing bikini on, shaded in the colour pink, but somehow this token attempt at femininity seemed to further highlight how the use of steroids and growth hormone abuse had turned her into a man in all but genitalia.

The venue had about five full-sized changing rooms and unlike at most of the shows I had done, you couldn't hear the roar of the crowd. I was relying on the calls from the backstage staff as I slowly started doing my pump-up. I was trying to keep calm but I could feel the excitement building inside me as I casually used my bands and started doing simple push-ups, then stopping to take on board more simple sugars to aid the pump.

The staff called out for the over-40s to take their place in line. I looked around me and there were about 15 people in my class. I felt nervous but I didn't feel outclassed. Yes, some of the guys were bigger, but the quality that I had certainly matched theirs.

As soon as I got on stage the size of the arena hit me. The noise was on a scale you would expect at a league football match and there must have been a few thousand people in the crowded aisles. I no longer felt nervous though as I strutted across the massive stage and hit my most muscular pose. The atmosphere was electric, the crowd responding to the impulsive pose-down by the competitors.

The MC called for us to fall into two lines. Somewhere even more over-40s bodybuilders had joined the line and now over 30 of the best bodybuilders in the world were on stage with me. We had to be split into two ranks because of the size of the class and I was taken through my compulsories along with about 14 other guys. It felt incredible being on that stage and it must have been adrenaline rushing through me because I was smashing through every pose.

There were many call-outs, I got two, but it soon became obvious that the judges had marked out their top six and as the contest went on they were just figuring out in what order they would finish. We were on stage for nearly an hour but it seemed to go in a heartbeat and I wished that I could have stayed in that moment, it felt so good. Granted I wasn't winning, but in a way I was already victorious because I had won my own personal battle with my health.

When I came off stage I didn't even bother taking my Dream Tan off. I ended up just aimlessly sat down backstage, watching Christina spread the chocolate-coloured tan over John. It was a strange scene, no one really said that much, just the odd word here and there. I handed John his bands and then started helping him pump up. I was looking around the room as the class three guys were called into line. It was a small class of about 15 guys and John looked on par with most of them.

Christina, Jo and I wished him good luck and then quickly went out into the crowded arena to watch him strut his stuff. His condition once again was flawless, but there were some massive physiques up against him. He posed Frank Zane-style, really emphasising his definition and symmetry, but once again the judges seemed in favour of the heavier muscled guys and John got edged out towards the end of the competition.

John wanted to stay backstage until the evening show as other people had done. They had set out their little camps, where circles of competitors relaxed among their compatriots and friends. The earlier frenzied activity had now been replaced with calmness. The battle had already been fought and now all that was left for the warriors was to go out and entertain the crowd and get their final placing when the evening show started.

I just wanted to get out and stretch my legs and explore the city, but most of all I wanted to have a nice fry-up. There were loads of cafés and we had lots of choices of different food, but the one I decided to go for after consulting with Jo was this nice-looking eatery about a mile from the venue. The only problem was that the owner didn't speak a word of English, yet Jo successfully ordered a complete English breakfast for me and burger and chips for her. I don't know if it was a good café or not but at that stage, after many months of restricting myself to mundane food, I was in heaven as I mixed forkfuls of bacon and egg together. We took our time walking back, just strolling and holding hands. I felt so relaxed, it seemed like we were just on holiday and not going back to take the stage at such a massive show.

The entrance hall to the venue was now in full flow and lines of stalls representing the leading brands of supplements and bodybuilding clothing were surrounded by a mass of people talking to some of the greats of our sport.

Dorian Yeats, probably the most famous of British bodybuilders, was there promoting his new company. He had taken the greatest title on the planet, Mr Olympia, and had won it an unbelievable six times. I would however like to apologise to him for my oversight that looked incredibly disrespectful, but was never meant. I was looking for some posters for Jo's brother Tom who has Down's syndrome, and who was very keen on bodybuilding. I don't know if I was slightly tired or my eyesight failed me but as we squeezed through the crowds to look at different posters I came across some of Dorian, who by now had been retired for a few years.

Jo prompted me to buy one, but me fearing that Tom only knew the most recent professionals, said: "Don't think he would know who he was!" Have you ever had that feeling when suddenly everyone stops talking at once and there is a deadly silence? As I turned to walk away, that's what happened, along with me suddenly realising that Dorian was actually there and he was now staring at my back. "That was Dorian sat there, wasn't it Jo?" I asked as I embarrassingly scuttled away, wishing the crowd would swallow me up. I could see by her smirking face that I was right. After that, I felt such an idiot for my faux pas that I kept well away from Dorian's trade stand.

We made our way backstage soon after that and I found out that there was going to be a parade before the evening show. Over 25 teams would take to the stage under the flag of the countries they represented. Unfortunately, but true at the time, the other nations were adorned in their official tracksuits and wore them with pride as they marched on to the stage to massive thunderous applause from the packed arena. They were closely followed by the British team in a mismatch of t-shirts and tracksuits. I even think John wore one with USA printed on it.

The evening show got underway. There were thousands of knowledgeable supporters and I don't think there was a spare seat in the whole auditorium. As expected we all got a chance to walk on and perform our mandatory poses.

My adrenaline was pumping like mad and when the MC shouted "Pose-down" I shot across the stage and got one of the main spots at the front. I knew that I hadn't made the top six, but I was going to milk this experience until every drop had gone. They left us posing and although there were a few jostles for space, the atmosphere was good-natured and the crowd were responding with loads of appreciation and urging us on.

I felt the light go out when they eventually stopped the pose-down. It seemed almost clinical the way they announced the top six and then a fleet of ladies came on to the stage to give the rest of us our medals. I found myself backstage, alone in my thoughts. The end had seemed to come so quickly and I could hear the final six competitors being taken through their comparisons.

I could feel the emotions swelling inside me. On one hand I wished that I could have done better, but in my heart I knew that I had taken an enormous journey, one that in my darkest hours I thought would have been impossible. The adrenaline that had kept me going had now seeped away. I was exhausted emotionally and physically, yet somehow I was in a place that seemed to have stopped still. I didn't even notice Jo until I felt her hug me and kiss me on the cheek. I smiled at her; I asked her if she thought Mike would have been watching.

I have to confess it was so emotional and overwhelming thinking that my friend had somehow been with me throughout the competitions. It is hard to imagine the depth of emotions that hit me. I really could sense his spirit and I could see his face and almost hear his words: "Bloody hell pal, what you upset about?" I smiled as I held Jo and in my mind I said to Mike: "Well old mate, we did it, we set out to get here, we did it!"

I was lost for ages in Jo's embrace. I guess I just wanted to stay there in that moment with the woman I loved, but eventually we went back to see John. He was busy pumping up and Christina was once again dutifully ensuring that she covered his physique and that the tan wasn't running.

Unfortunately John didn't make the top six either. It was a fantastic show with top-class competitors and the star of the British team was Bernie who was given a much disputed second place.

I was completely knackered by the time we got back to the hotel and I just wanted to be alone with Jo so I turned down John's offer to go out for a bite to eat. I just collapsed on the bed and chatted to Jo until she fell asleep. I could hear her gentle breath in the silence of the room as I tried to sleep.

In some ways I just wanted the story to end there like in films where the actor accomplishes his goal and the film titles start to roll across the screen, but this is true life and I woke up early the next day and scraped my weary body off the comfy bed, threw cold water over my face and woke Jo up at the ungodly hour of 4.30am to join the rest of the guys in squeezing into this small bloody coach and I wouldn't have minded that they had picked us up at 5am but our flight didn't leave until 2pm.

All you could hear throughout the hour-long journey to the train station was moaning, snoring, farting and more moaning. It resembled a scene from the *Night of the Living Dead* as the sleep-deprived, hungry and disorientated bodybuilders staggered from the coach and walked wearily to the train station. It was eerie and somewhat surreal, our voices echoing around the deserted platforms. The station was vast and to depleted bodybuilders like me it felt like a labyrinth.

I had no sense of direction, in fact it was all I could do to plod behind the others as I was so knackered and cold. John was our intrepid leader and at one stage he shouted back to the group that he had found the right train and beckoned me on. It was with great reluctance that we finally vacated the comfy seats that we had found when the girls informed us that the train was going to Berlin and not Cologne!

Eventually one of the other guys found the right train, but at that stage I would have gone to Berlin if I could have sat down in a warm place. I don't remember much of the trip, all I can recall is Jo nudging me and saying we were there.

I was suddenly pitched back into life as the beautiful colours of the Christmas market of Cologne greeted us and even at such an early hour, the place was in full swing. The backdrop of the cathedral resembled a picture postcard. We had lots of time before we had to make our way to the airport so it was nice to stroll around the local vicinity, even though it was so cold.

The market square was full of German cuisine; the aroma of freshly prepared food filled the air and littered around the square were even more places to dine and to a bodybuilder who hadn't eaten nice food for about 30 weeks, it was paradise! I immediately located a familiar fast food shop and set about having my breakfast; two double cheeseburgers with fries. It was an amazing place to walk around. It reinvigorated me and Jo and we went sight-seeing, Jo looking for mementoes and presents and me scavenging for food. Several presents and another seven or eight burgers later and it was finally time to meet up with the rest of the guys.

My heart dropped when we got to the airport as apart from my British team-mates, there had been some delays and there were queues all over the place. I don't know to this day if it was a ploy on John's part or he had some kind of panic attack but he just collapsed and I had to hold on to him to keep him upright. The staff came over to see us and after being reassured he was okay to fly, they took us to the head of the queue. I found it ironic that Jo was searched yet again when they had two bodybuilders, full of the remains of false tan and looking like zombies dressed in tan-soiled t-shirts and baggies in front of them, looking really dodgy.

At the airport to greet us when we got home were the paparazzi, banners displaying the words "Welcome Home British Team", and supporters fighting for a glimpse of their heroes! No, this is bodybuilding, so there was nothing, just the people who loved us and in retrospect we all had given so much we didn't want a fuss, we just wanted to go home, sleep and eat.

Time to rebuild

A COUPLE OF weeks later, *Bella* magazine sent a photographer around to the house to take what we thought were a few pictures. It was after about three hours of trying to smile in tandem that Jo and I finally thought the money wasn't worth trying to push out yet another cheesy grin.

I think they thought I would still be in shape, so they took me to Silvers and wanted me to pose. I had somewhat indulged and was about two stone heavier and Jo was laughing at me until she realised they wanted her to pose, draping herself seductively around me. It would be another two hours amid much laughter from the guys at the gym before they got a photograph that they were happy with.

I was looking forward to the magazine coming out until I saw the pictures. We didn't look seductive, we looked terrified and the write-up was straight out of a Mills and Boon novel. It depicted me as some sort of muscular Romeo and Jo as my Juliet who swooned when she saw my muscular biceps. It gave our friends, guys at the gym and our loved ones enough material to laugh at for ages and Jo said she would rather go and show her arse in Tesco than ever do it again.

It was back to the humdrum of off-season training for me and I learnt that my training partner Ian had successfully applied to join the Royal Navy, so I was back on my own again. I contemplated retiring throughout this time. The adrenaline had driven me through everything and now in the cold light of day I realised that although my year had been a success, what lay before me was two to three years of hard graft and I had serious doubts about whether my body, that was now showing the effects of what I had dragged it through, could stand it.

Everyone seemed stoked up by what the local papers were calling an amazing comeback and to be honest the hype had carried me through, but now my body was reminding me that I owed it big time. I needed space, I didn't want to be around anyone, I had to let my body heal and let it become human again. I was relieved to be off the gear. The short-acting steroids that we use before a competition had forced me to inject more often and my body had felt like some kind of overworked effigy doll.

I kept out of Silvers and used another gym. I knew my friends were pumped about what John and I had achieved but I just wanted to go and have some leisurely training sessions. I seriously thought that my competition days were through and I felt happy to stroll around the gym and take it easy. The slippers and pipe of retirement seemed to be beckoning me but after a few weeks of this I could feel it again. It was a mixture of dread and elation and I realised that I was inadvertently stepping up the intensity and the addiction was still alive and well.

By the time I returned to Silvers I was hungry, I wanted to do it all over again, but this time I wanted a top placing at the Universe. There was no shortage of training partners either as guys were now lining up to train with me, thinking that all they had to do was turn up and they would get success, but after a few weeks they would start making excuses and I sort of resigned myself to training on my own.

I thought when Terry approached and asked to train with me that he would be like the others. He wasn't even a bodybuilder, he was into martial arts, but what made him stand out from the other guys was that he was hungry to change his physique and he was used to hard graft because the job he worked in meant that he spent his working week lifting and erecting heavy headstones in his father's funeral business.

The workouts were becoming gruelling. My joints were creaking and I couldn't even lie in bed without pain. I was constantly having to use an anti-inflammatory drug called diclofenac to try to give me some respite, but even turning over in bed hurt my elbows and getting up in the morning was a major chore. It had become like some major Army tactical manoeuvre. Sometimes I would have to hook my right leg over the side of the mattress to pull me closer to the edge and push myself slowly up to a seated position. I would then rise slowly and begin stretching exercises to try to prepare my lower back, not for training, but for shaving and brushing my teeth at the bathroom sink.

The leg sessions were also becoming evil. I was squatting seven 20kg plates a side on the machine, leg-pressing 15 plates a side for eight to 12 reps and then finishing off with hack squats until I couldn't move the weight anymore, then I would get my training partner to help me up with it and slowly lowering it down on my own as a negative rep.

We started going to a well-known gym in Middleton and we were joined by Kris from the gym. It was typical of its type; some machines had been made for use by its owner, a former world champion. We would use the squat machine there, piling weight on each side until we couldn't move. It sometimes felt like your knees would burst through the wraps and catapult themselves across the gym. We used to test how hard we had worked because they had two old

Chesterfield sofas that sank when you sat in them and you ended up inches off the floor. The first test was to see how easy you could stand back up; I swear at times that sofa was harder to use than the hack squat. The second one was to see if you could navigate the two flights of uneven steps that descended sharply from the gym entrance without falling over.

We devised workouts and went out to beat each other; my body was so sore that at times even combing my hair hurt. I used to creak when I got up in the morning. My elbows, back and knee joints all protested about the gruelling regime I was putting them through.

At times I would be moving so painfully, people would come up and ask if I was alright. I remember once when I had applied for a course at the local college I was making my way gingerly up the stairs the day after a leg workout and the cleaner, who seemed quite concerned, approached and took me aside. I wondered what was wrong and then she quietly informed me that there was a lift and a disabled toilet if I needed it.

Apart from feeling my body wrecking, my general health had improved and although I had some days when I had to retire to bed early, I was managing my lifestyle quite well. It was during this time I started work again as a support worker. I was employed in Oldham working with guys who had all sorts of disabilities and issues. Some clients had Alzheimer's, some had MS and others had mental health problems. My job entailed taking folk out and doing activities such as gardening or going to the cinema. I enjoyed the gardening with the chap with Alzheimer's. Sometimes it felt more like a treasure hunt because our digging would reveal household items that he had previously hidden and forgotten.

The gym work was going well; I used every rep to take me closer to where I wanted to be. I was aware of people training around me but in some ways they didn't exist. My whole being was in that last forced repetition that made my body shake but took me closer to my dream. Most people go to the gym to keep fit or as part of a social life but to competitive bodybuilders it is work, and mind-numbing intensity day after day. It is like you have two jobs; one is an eight-hour shift and the other is one to two hours of inhumane graft. You leave the gym with nothing, all you want to do is eat and sleep.

It's showtime

B Y 2008 I knew I had improved enough to compete again. I had selected the shows I was doing. I wasn't going to do any warming-up shows. I selected the EPF Open British and the NAC British championships.

Terry was still as enthusiastic, he had gained around two stone with me and he came up with the idea of dieting with me with a view to doing a local competition. It was good to have him with me especially when in the cardio room, but even Terry had his limits and it was after about six weeks that he informed me that he couldn't "hack" the diet. I tried to reassure him that it was not a failure on his part, that many people set out to compete but few actually end up on stage. His encouragement and dedication was still there though and he helped me drive through the pain and doubt that has accompanied me throughout my competitive career.

Two weeks out I saw Ben as usual. I was holding a little bit of body fat and water on my lower back but he assured me I was spot on target. I found myself every few hours, no matter where I was, just casually lifting my top up and pinching the skin fold, but no matter what I did it seemed to be the same. It become a compulsion. I even ended up doing it in my sleep.

On the day of the EPF show, Terry, Al from the gym and Jo travelled down to the Midlands with me. Al had just finished his competition and was in the throes of eating everything in sight. We arrived in Halesowen and decided to go for a coffee. Al was soon stuffing his face. I swear there was no time during that day he wasn't eating.

We had to wait for the show to get started and we found a table where they could sit and I could lay down on the floor with my legs elevated across one of the chairs. I know it sounds masochistic but I loved the fact that I could feel the floor painfully pressing against my back because it meant there was very little body fat left there. However it didn't stop me from going to the toilet every few minutes to either check my lower back or to urinate once more.

When we were called backstage, the guy in charge said Jo couldn't come into the male changing rooms with me, so Al ended up coming back to help me. I felt relaxed until he said: "Jim you're not tanned enough," and then I panicked and my back started to go into spasm. I was in agony and had to lie down as I watched Al go out the door to see if he could get some more tan. I was lying there watching the other guys prepare. There were five of them, all well known and looking good. Al eventually came back and said Jo had bought some Dream Tan and he set about helping me to my feet.

I was in pain just standing there, letting Al tan me up, and I thought there was no way that I could compete. I looked in the mirror and saw that I was cut, I was ready, I was now in the best shape of my life and all I had to do was to put the pain aside and get my arse on that stage and beat them.

I did some light warm-up exercises to get some blood in my body and took some diclofenac. I had a choice; I could go home or put on the "fixed smile" and get my arse out there. I finished off the red wine, took a swig of whisky and looked for the special flapjacks Jo had made for me and I just grabbed a handful of them and forced them down. Al was instantly there, like a trusty hound, his eyes pleading for any leftovers, but after all the dieting he had done I couldn't deny him.

I left him the remaining few and started to slowly do some press-ups and isometrics using my rubber bands. I had this vision that I would just go into a pose and my back would go into complete spasm, but as we were called to line up to go backstage I knew that the only way I was going home was either by being carried off stage or with a trophy in my hand. I got the first call-out and my mind was saying take it easy, but I knew with the quality these guys had I would have to give everything. "Double bicep," the MC called out, and I instantly tensed my quads and every sinew I had as I raised my arms above my head and bent them, clenching my fists and my teeth into a smile that masked the pain I could feel.

They really worked us hard, but as I was posing, my back was becoming slightly easier. I don't know if it was the alcohol, diclofenac or just shear adrenaline, but I knew I was going to make it through to the end. After the pose-down we were called to the back of the stage. We were all exhausted, but still kept "tight" which is bodybuilding speak for keeping the physique tensed.

They gave medals to two of the guys and I looked at the two left, they had top-class physiques, and whatever placing I got I would be happy with it. You stand there on stage, shaking from the effort that you are putting into keeping your body flexed and displaying a "confident smile", and the MC seems to take an age to present the placing, but eventually he announced that I had won the EPF Masters. I felt an incredible relief; I kissed the trophy, the adrenaline rush now masking any leftover pain. Jo and my mates came rushing backstage. All I could think of was that I wanted some nice food, but unfortunately I had to share my after-show goodies with my ever-hungry mate Al. I think we even shared Opal Fruits that Jo found when everything else had been eaten.

When we got back to the flat I went straight into the kitchen and started munching on some of the goodies Jo had bought for me. It was about 3.30am, when a gap in my feeding frenzy appeared, that I thought: "Jim where are your manners?" I promptly cut a nice wedge of the cheesecake I was about to demolish and took it into the bedroom to wake the now fast asleep Jo. She eventually awoke, looking startled and I think she politely refused it. Actually I think her words were slightly stronger if I remember rightly.

The next show was the NAC Masters so I was back in the gym the next night after work in the cardio room and pedalling, my lonely mind and bum-numbing journey on the stationary bike. I was now doing HIIT training as well, which meant that I would introduce all-out sprints at different intervals. It would go something like this: sprint for a minute, then slow down and try to recover and then sprint again. The sessions didn't last long but while they were on they were brutal!

The cardio room at Silvers is a very isolated place; it had just one window that looks out into the reception area and most of the time that I used it I would be on my own. I could see people passing, laughing and being "human". At times I felt like a zoo animal, performing on his bike for spectators that passed by the window and on the front of my "cage" it had the words: "Do Not Feed the Animal."

It is in this state of mind that you sometimes question your sanity, people will say things like "the show is only a week away so it is all downhill now", but when you are so depleted every minute is counted, every waking night when you are either too hungry, nervous with excitement or simply urinating every few minutes due to water manipulation.

It feels like hell on Earth and the only salvation is the precious few minutes that you are on stage in the best shape of your life. That is what competitive bodybuilders live for, those precious few moments in the light when people get to see the finished product.

On the morning of the NAC show I knew that I was even more cut and weighing in at over 13 stone. I knew that the guys from the gym would be there and for the first time in my life I began to feel pressure. In most of the competitions I had done I had been the underdog but now there was an expectation from people that I would win. I travelled the few miles to the venue at Middleton, with Jo and my number one fan, Tom, who is Jo's brother. He used to accompany me to Silvers on a Sunday, he loved bodybuilding and despite having Down's syndrome wanted nothing else than to one day be on the stage of a bodybuilding show.

I felt at home at the NAC. I knew that my brother and all my friends including Ben, my mentor, would be there to cheer me on. I spotted Joe, the owner of Silvers, his long blonde hair standing out in the crowd, but I didn't want to be around people. I wanted to just get on the stage and then do the business. As soon as I could I got backstage, Jo came with me, and I knew we wouldn't have to wait as we were on first. I looked around me and saw some familiar faces, a couple of the guys were from the EPF show and then I saw Bill, he had a top-quality physique and he was in shape. There were five guys in total in my line-up and I knew this was going to be both a physical and psychological battle.

Jo began to tan me up, I felt tense though, I didn't want to let anyone down and I had gone from feeling confident to doubting myself within a few minutes. As I started my pre-pump ritual, trying to get as much chocolate down me as possible and topping myself up with the red wine, I could hear the others frantically pumping up and I looked across at Bob. He was definitely my rival for the title, his back looked huge and full. He had very few weaknesses.

I started pumping up, willing myself to take my time and not exhaust myself through pumping up too much and then having little or no energy to pose with. It is another world backstage, competitions can be won and lost, it's easy to get carried away by the adrenaline and start warming up too early which can mean that you end up totally fatigued before you've even gone on stage. Psychological games are played, we all did this to each other as we vied for time in front of the mirror and hit different poses. It is fascinating to watch the different approaches of athletes; some are very loud, even aggressive, some just go about their business quietly.

We were called to line up and this was it, I wanted to win so badly so I could get another Universe invitation and this time try to make the top six. It soon became obvious from the call-outs that it was between me and Bill and I could tell he wanted this as much as me. I could hear him grunting, putting every fibre of his being into each and every pose. There were few call-outs and I think we were all glad under the heated lights of the stage. They gave the medals out to the fourth- and fifth-placed guys and the three of us stood, keeping "tight" as they gave the third-placed trophy to one of the guys who had competed with me at the EPF.

I could taste the tension in the air as Bill and I stood for an age awaiting their verdict and once again, I heard the beautiful words: "Jim Moore is your Masters winner." I had done it, I had not only qualified, I was going there as the champion. Jo was waiting backstage for me and I hugged her, once again covering her in false tan, but I don't think either of us cared. I was overcome with emotion as I fought back tears of Joy.

Eugene, who managed the shows, came back to see me. "You're doing the overall aren't you Jim?" he asked. Eugene was a great guy, a former champion himself who had his own gym and had built this show up from scratch. I was so euphoric that I agreed, although I felt totally knackered and could feel my nemesis, the sciatica, coming on. Ben came up to me and said I looked the best I had since my car crash in 2002. He bought me a flapjack from one of the supplement stalls that promote their wares at shows and we strolled back to take our seats with my friends and family.

The "overall" is at the end of the night, where all the winners of the individual classes get together and vie to be voted best in the show. I had fun doing it, but I was well aware that the heavyweight, Robbie, was top-class and the big guys usually win the title. The arena was emptying when we came on stage. There were bodybuilders of all different ages and sizes but in the end Robbie was justifiably given the overall title to much applause from the crowd. We had a team picture taken as we were the guys who would represent our country at the Universe.

I was just coming back off stage when I heard a massive roar from the crowd who were left in the hall and then shouts, mixed with laughter. At first I thought it was for Robbie who we had left on stage having some pictures taken on his own, but I was wrong. I looked around the curtain and I had to smile. Tom, Jo's brother, had climbed on to the stage and at first I was alarmed that people would take the piss out of him, but I was wrong. The atmosphere was great, people were shouting and encouraging him and the little bugger was milking it. He had stripped off his top and he was now hitting all the poses that I had taught him.

The crowd really loved it and by the big smile on his face, I could see that Tom loved it too and after hitting his "most muscular pose" which is the climax of my routine, he waved and bowed to his captive audience.

We left the venue together and went home. Just one week to go and I would be at the Universe in Germany and in the best shape of my life. I woke up the next morning after a night of feasting and as I stood up, my luck ran out. I felt like someone had lumbar-punched me. I was in agony and the only place I could fall was the floor. Jo had gone to work and I couldn't move; my back had gone into full spasm. I think I developed Tourette's Syndrome as I painstakingly crawled along the floor. The bed came into view, it was now even hurting me when I breathed, I could feel cold sweat on my back with the effort of trying to move. I must have laid there for ages before I summoned up the courage to get on the bed.

My body was shaking as though I had done a workout with all-out intensity. I lay on the bed, breathing heavily, looking at the ceiling and I knew in my heart that I was in trouble. I couldn't even move to make a phone call and it wasn't until Jo came in that we were able to call out the doctor. She gave me an injection of diclofenac and although the pain was slightly less, I felt emotional, I knew that fate had raised her hand and taken my chance away from me. It was with a heavy heart that I contacted Eugene and told him that I would not be able to go to the Universe.

They say that people eat for comfort, and after that I felt so depressed and immobile that by the end of the week I had learnt all the telephone numbers of the local takeaways that deliver. I think I became their favourite customer. It was both a happy and sad moment to learn that Bill, who had finished second to me, had gone to the Universe and finished fourth.

Beefing it

CHRISTMAS WAS around the corner and I was still continuing my feasting. My weight by the New Year had ballooned up to over 17 stone and it felt terrible. I remember having to take a trip to Manchester and I met John at the tram station in Bury, he bought me a coffee and as we were talking I noticed one of my shoelaces had come loose. The next few minutes were filled with me breathing like someone making a rude phone call and John laughing.

I tried to get down on one knee with dignity but abandoned that when I realised that I was now panting as though I was giving birth. It was the equivalent of a climber reaching the summit of Mount Everest when I finally reached my destination. With the laces tied, I had to grab hold of John to slowly pull myself back up.

I was beginning to think if bodybuilding didn't work out for me, I just could carry on eating and try sumo wrestling instead. I knew that the weight would fall off once I was into hardcore training and I was back on my off-season diet so shortly after that I looked at a plan to compete at the NABBA North West and try to qualify for the British Finals in May 2010. I was still working in Oldham and I had developed a good rapport with the clients. The job suited me as I was out and about most days and they definitely weren't boring. Owen had MS. He had been a keen biker in his time, but he was now confined to a wheelchair. He was a real character and I was told that before he had become totally immobile, he had gone just about everywhere on his disability scooter.

I was with him one time. We had been dropped off near the Manchester Science Museum. I was shocked to see so many people lining the route and it became obvious that something was happening. The museum wasn't open and a nearby policeman informed us that Prince Charles and Camilla were visiting and that the museum would be open shortly after their visit. There was a wall-to-wall police presence and after speaking to Owen, we decided to find a place to have a coffee and come back when it was all over.

I pushed the modified wheelchair along the cobbled street and I didn't get more than a few more yards before disaster struck. One of the front wheels collapsed. I managed to steady the chair and all I could see were hordes of people getting more and more excited as the royal visitors were coming out and I couldn't move.

There next thing we knew, as we looked around for help, was that a number of "suited" guys had surrounded us and started questioning us. They closely inspected the wheelchair and did a name check. Owen was loving all the fuss but I could just see the television news headlines: "Terrorist threat to royal visit", and then panning to the picture of me desperately trying to tell them Owen wasn't answering their questions, not because he was a terrorist but because he had MS and couldn't speak. It couldn't have been more than a few minutes of interrogation but to me it seemed to last an age until eventually they realised that this was an unfortunate event and they offered to lift the wheelchair with me to a local café, where I telephoned for assistance to get us back home.

The time had come to go back on the gear. My recent successes had put me in contact with a new guy who supplied gear to a lot of competitors and the bonus with this guy was that he lived near me and would often drop it off to me outside my flat. He would phone me to say he was on his way and I would wait outside for him like a kid waiting for the ice cream man. Sometimes he would meet me and some other guys near where he lived and he would have the boot of his car up while we waited in line to be served.

I remember once I needed some primobolin which is a fast-acting steroid used mainly for pre-competition as it holds very little water. It was also as rare as rocking horse shit but this guy had the real stuff though unfortunately for me he had just sold the last ten vials to the guy in front of me. He turned and shouted to the other bloke that we both knew who by now was across the street mingling with the general public: "Hey Pete, do you really need that primobolin because Jim is competing in another couple of weeks?"

I couldn't believe he had shouted it out and people were now looking over at the small queue of colourfully-clad bodybuilders grouped suspiciously around his Volvo waiting to "buy an ice cream".

I was constantly being advised to use growth hormone. For me it felt like I was stepping over a line in the sand because I had previously vowed never to use it, but I had seen so many guys have major successes by combining it with steroid use. So after much deliberation and many weeks of mental turmoil, I succumbed and I bought my first course of growth hormone in the hope that this would add the finishing touches to my physique. It had to be injected into the stomach, so the injection part didn't feel bad, but I did fear the "growth belly". This is a side-effect of the drug that it pushes the stomach out. You must have seen some of the pro bodybuilders that when they are relaxed their body fat is very low but they look like pregnant women.

It was with trepidation I used it, but from the first few injection I noticed that my abdominals looked more defined. Over the forthcoming months I noticed that my physique had filled out and I looked bigger but leaner too. Even at 16 stone I was looking sharp and stronger than ever in the gym, but I had a slight problem. Well I thought it was a slight problem, but this was going to come back and haunt me a year later. I was getting a lot of indigestion and having problems eating food due to the acid reflux, but when you are driven, these things don't count, all that you see is the "prize".

A new gym had opened up near me. I loved training at Silvers but the parking was restricted and for convenience, I started using the Olympia gym on my way home from work. Some people had warned me it was full of young guys with an "attitude". Granted, like all gyms, it had its share of characters. There were fighters, both legal and illegal, and you could spot the rogues, the guys who hang around gyms to build themselves up in order to "front" their "business".

I was in the changing rooms once when a young guy told me he was having problems training his legs because he had got injured and he showed me his thigh, which had a cup-size scar and within it was a more smaller circular indentation. It took me a while to realise the "injury" was in fact a bullet wound. Lots of hardcore gyms have their share of guys who are into gang life and activities, but mostly the Olympia gym was full of people working their arses off to improve their physiques, so for me it had a good atmosphere.

Ask no questions get told no lies as my mate who worked the doors used to say, let them do their gangster work and we'll just do what we do. I learnt long ago to not talk to people in the gym on any level other than training.

The more you get involved with certain people, the more you get drawn into a life that you might not want to be in.

The only thing that gets on my nerves is this new phenomenon of people who take their mobile phones into the gym and spend ages chatting on them. Gyms are there for training in for fuck's sake, you shouldn't have the energy to make a phone call, never mind hogging the bench press and gabbing away for 20 minutes! If it was up to me you would have to hand them in at reception like a gun-slinger going into a western town that had to hand his guns into the local sheriff on arrival and then they would only be returned when they left town.

Taking it to the max

IN JANUARY of 2010 I started my cut. I was very lean to begin with and I knew that I could take my time and slowly get ripped while keeping the new muscle gains I had made. I was training with high intensity and unlike other times even eight weeks into the conditioning work, I was feeling strong. I kept the carbohydrates higher than I had done previously. I was still 15 stones and five pounds and unbelievably I had pretty low body fat. I was giving it everything in every session. I never believed in lowering the weights when on a diet, I kept everything as heavy as possible and only adjusted it if my body couldn't use the weight with proper form.

The Olympia gym had some teething problems with the electrics and now and again the lights would fuse. I was training on my own just a few weeks before the North West. The diet was now getting to me, I was tired, but you still have to give everything. I had four plates a side on the hack machine after doing sets of leg presses and squats. I could hear myself scream with the exertion of fighting out the last few reps and then it happened, total blackness; the lights had gone out in the gym.

I heard myself swear out loud as the weight of the hack squat took me down to the bottom like a sack of spuds. I sat there, exhausted, thinking why the fuck don't they sort out these bleeding lights and then I realised the lights hadn't fused, I must have done. The only light that had gone out was the one in my head. It wasn't the first time I had collapsed under a weight through feeling faint. To the outside world they wouldn't understand the desperation you feel when trying to take your body to the limit.

My social skills had also gone. The only person I could converse with was Joe, the owner of Silvers, who after many years of saying he wanted to compete had chosen to do the over-40s at the same show as me. He would phone me up and run things by me and ask my advice. His ability to hold down a decent conversation was as bad as mine and in a way, it felt good to hear that I wasn't the only one suffering.

I was so bad that in my last session before the NABBA show I couldn't talk to anyone at all. The normal jovial me had long since gone. It just took too much effort to reply to people. I had finished my workout and I knew the girls on reception would be their usual chatty selves and I didn't want to appear unsociable but I just wanted to escape and not have to make chit-chat. I waited until they had turned their backs and were stacking the shelves up and lowering my head, I quickly ran past reception into the street.

I didn't know why but I felt rough, worse than I had ever felt, I would go to bed early and not even feel like being close to Jo. I felt like I was dying as I tried to digest food and drink 12 litres of water. I thought it was nerves that made me feel so low and I knew from experience that I just had to hang in there. I don't know how I worked until the day before, I actually can't remember much of it, only eating and urinating all the time.

On the day of the show we arrived early as usual and Joe phoned. He sounded as rough as I felt and we arranged to meet outside the venue. Having some time to fill, Jo and I strolled across the road to the nearest pub. I felt like some kind of alien species as everyone turned and looked at the white lad with the orange tan.

As we came out of the pub, we saw the lads from the gym across the road. Joe was there too, he looked nervous and slightly agitated, but I knew that by his haggard, sunken-faced look that he was in shape. Eventually the doors opened and all the competitors got called up to the reception area to sign in.

There were six competitors in my line-up and Joe's class had seven. NABBA is a top-quality show and always attracts the best guys so I didn't even bother looking at any of the names on the sheet. I turned around and then I saw him, he had tan on his face which meant he was competing. Walter O'Malley. Nearly 25 years had passed since as a nervous young guy, I had taken my first faltering steps into his gym and now I was going to be competing in the same show as the former Mr Universe. I went up to him and shook his hand straight away. I was suddenly energised, I couldn't believe it. Walter always had time for everyone. I am not sure though if he truly remembered me but he was far too much of a gentleman to say so.

A number of us went backstage, friends from the gym, Joe, his girlfriend Wendy and my Jo. The juniors were first on, then the under-21s, Joe would be on next and then the over-50s straight after. It felt good backstage. I was so tired though, I could have gone to sleep. Joe went on stage before I started tanning up. I could hear the crowd cheering and I looked in the mirror, I was ripped and weighing 14 stone 7lbs. I knew I was at my best and I would need to be as the quality of the guys I was up against stood out.

These guys might be 50, but many had spent their entire lives competing with NABBA. One of them, Gordon, had won titles at junior, Mr and over-40s. We were called to the side of the stage just in time to see that Joe had finished third and he had qualified for the British Championships, which were in two weeks.

I couldn't believe it when Walter lined up with us. There was only one over-60s competitor and they had put Walter with the over-50s line-up. It was a privilege to stand next to him on stage and the crowd were going wild; this group of "old men" stood before them, muscular, cut and looking much younger than their years.

We then were told to go backstage and do our own individual posing routines. I was on after Gordon. I walked to the centre of the stage and my music started. The theme from *Pulp Fiction* blasted out, but unfortunately in the intro there is some swearing. I started to move through my usual poses but no applause came, just a deadly silence that hung above the music, then some shouts of "go on Jim" and as I concluded, a polite ripple of applause.

There were no call-outs, we just stood in line and before the mandatories were called out, they made an announcement: "NABBA does not allow any swearing to be used in any posing music, competitors doing this can be deducted points and if they continue to do so will be banned."

I felt myself mouthing the words "oh fuck"! I had made a rookie mistake and not checked out their rules. I felt slightly shaken but started to grind out the mandatory poses. You could hear the guys grunt as they pushed themselves under the fierce heat of the stage lights. At the conclusion, they lined us up in different positions; I was now next to Gordon on my right, with another guy called David on my left.

Only three line-outs were called before the MC shouted "pose-down". I stood alongside Walter and hit my best poses and the music seemed to go on for ages. We had started out with gusto, striking each movement with all-out intent; now though, we were beginning to wilt and after about another two minutes, when all the competitors were waving the white flag, they ordered us to the back of the stage.

Walter was awarded the title of over-60s winner and then medals were given to three of the guys. It left David, Gordon and me. David was given third place and much to my disappointment, they finally gave Gordon the title to much shouting and applause.

I had qualified and although it would have been good to win it, the results meant that I would have to improve and be harder to beat at the finals. I went back to the main arena where my brother had arrived with his wife Hannah and they were really upbeat, but I felt tired and low. Joe was celebrating as for someone to qualify at the North West in their first ever show was a major achievement. I didn't feel like the day had been a success for me and rather than putting a downer on the party-like atmosphere, I ended up sneaking off with my brother, Hannah and Jo to the local fish and chip shop to have steak pudding and chips, but I still felt rough and struggled to eat it. When I got home, I was looking forward to eating the goodies Jo had bought but I just ended up going to bed instead.

I spoke with Ben again and it was our intention to introduce more carbs into the diet and with only two weeks to go we wanted to ensure we didn't deplete any more. I was struggling to eat though; the acid reflux seemed to be getting worse. I was taking Gaviscon and that seemed to ease it a little, but I was paranoid about using any medication because it may have made me retain water.

Joe and I had decided to do the Mr International at Pendle Valley the week after and when we arrived, it was one of the most beautiful days of the year; the sun was shining and the guys from the gym were sunbathing as we arrived. The atmosphere felt relaxed as we all chatted outside the venue, before going in to sign up for our classes. The guys were drinking at the bar and Joe and I were necking our red wine concoction. By the time we were on stage, a few of the guys were quite drunk, as were both Joe and myself.

I had finished my half bottle of wine and Joe had brought extra. Having not drunk all year except for the half bottle at the North West, I felt maybe a bit too relaxed and was laughing and joking with the lads before I realised that I was on in the next few minutes. After quickly doing a few lop-sided press-ups and half-hearted bicep curls with my training bands, I somewhat unsteadily started posing on stage. There were three guys against me. I can't recall much, but remember that in the free posing round, just as I was rising to hit the crescendo of my new music, 'Firestarter', Daz, one of the guys from the gym, drunkenly stood up and shouted: "Hope there's no swearing in this one Jim." I couldn't help but laugh as I went through my usual routine.

I don't know if it was because I was slightly drunk but for once I was the epitome of grace and style and I flowed from one pose to another, but remember this was from my perspective, sober members of the audience may have disagreed. It was totally unprofessional but somehow the day seemed to be a time for chilling before the NABBA finals the week after. Much to my surprise and delight, as the proceedings for the over-50s came to a close, I was awarded the title.

The prize for the overall was a nice-looking sword and it turned out to be between four of us. We walked on and they quickly took us through the mandatories. For some bloody reason though after they called for a side chest pose. I think they went out for a brew because they kept us holding the pose for ages. I could feel my body shaking with the effort and I could hear the younger guys behind me, gasping and grunting too. I looked over to the judges who were arguing. Three minutes went by, no decision and then I lost it, and I could hold the pose no more.

I looked at them. Was this test of endurance to see whoever gave up first lost? I was about to say: "Do you guys know how old I am or have you got a bleeding insurance policy on me?" and then I spotted that they had brought the guest poser up to seek his advice.

It seemed there was a hung vote between me and one of the other guys and after about a five-minute delay, with the other guys still struggling to hold their "statuesque-like" side chests, they finally awarded the overall to the other bloke. After all the exertion I was just happy to go home, well not straight home, we did call at Kentucky Fried Chicken on the way. I had never tried it before but friends had told me it tasted great. I couldn't wait to sample it and Jo drove me up to the drive-thru window.

I hadn't a clue what to order but I had heard that you could buy a bucket, so I ended up ordering a 16-piece bucket. I was shocked when it came; I had expected 16 nugget-sized pieces, not whole pieces of chicken. I was hungry though and thought I would eat them but once again as soon as I had digested a few, the pain shot through my body. It was indigestion again and it made me feel so bad that I ended up having some Gaviscon to wash it down with and then went to bed.

I woke up on Monday, just six days before the finals. It was time to manipulate the water and I began the process of drinking excessive amounts but everything seemed to affect my stomach and this was more apparent when on the Wednesday I tried to carb up.

It was not going well and after four meals of complex carbs of oats and potatoes, I'd had enough. I couldn't take any more. My stomach was retching and the acid reflux felt like it was ripping my chest apart. Even when I tried to sleep, despite copious amounts of Gaviscon, the pain was keeping me awake. I was worried, not about what the problem was as I had never heard of anyone dying from heartburn, I was more worried that my weight was plummeting and I couldn't get enough food down to stop it.

Finally Friday arrived and I had arranged to stay in a hotel in Southport, so I could be there to sign in at 10am on the Saturday. It was a family-run hotel and a few of the other competitors were staying there too. One of the figure ladies, Anita, was booking in when we arrived and arranged to have steak for breakfast. It was about 7pm on a beautiful summer night that Jo and I sat outside drinking glasses of dry white wine. It felt so relaxing despite the sharp pain I had through drinking the wine, to just watch the world go by and it must have been around 10pm before we retired to our room to sleep.

Despite feeling a little drunk, which I hoped would relax me and enable me to get some shut-eye, I had the usual erratic pre-show night and I woke early around 6am and went into the bathroom to look at my reflection. The wine had done its job. I was not only ripped but bone dry too, and my weight was only just above 13st 7lb. I had lost over a stone since the North West and knew some of it must have been muscle fibre, but I could do little about it now and the show must go on.

Jo woke up at 8am and gave me a further coat of tan. It really did emphasise just how low my body fat was, but I knew that from just walking there was so little fat on my feet that even moving hurt. I couldn't even sit for long because my arse and lower back had no cushion of fat on them either.

I went down for breakfast and I wished that I had ordered a steak for breakfast too because trying to shell seven boiled eggs, with tanned fingers, wasn't a good idea. The eggs looked purple in colour due to being stained by my hands but I didn't care, I just wanted to get them down despite the indigestion I was feeling.

When we reached the venue, Joe was waiting outside, and everyone looked tense. This was the climax of many years of training and dieting and everything was now in the hands of the judges.

The over-40s were allowed to go backstage but I was stopped, and they informed me that I would have to wait another 20 minutes before my class would be able to go backstage. I explained that I had to go back as soon as possible because I was tanning my friend Joe up and they informed me that there were two ladies who were there to help competitors with their tan.

Security was strict alright, only competitors were allowed backstage and despite my protests, it was another 25 minutes before I was able to go through and then I had to go past a number of security personnel who looked down a list of names before allowing me to finally reach backstage.

I saw Joe, who looked worried. There may have been two ladies helping but when you're tense and the "helpers" have so many people to assist, it doesn't do your nerves any favours having to wait around like that. I told him that I couldn't believe how strict they were and we joked that the trophies must have been made of gold and worth a bloody fortune. The only thing missing from the scene was armed uniformed guards with snarling Alsatians.

It was as I was helping Joe tan up that the back doors were suddenly opened by a well-known competitor. He didn't bring just a guy in to help him tan up, he brought a whole bloody tanning booth complete with all the equipment! It took up loads of space and some of the other guys were grumbling and reluctantly making room for it. Someone must have informed security though, because they came rushing backstage shouting: "Who's got a bloody tanning booth?" Then they saw who was being tanned and just said "don't make a mess" as they simply turned away and ignored this violation of the rules.

It seemed that security was very "selective", but there was no point in getting annoyed about it as some of them did. I just ignored all the fuss and carried on applying some Muscle Sheen that we had bought to add a final touch and make the cuts look even more prominent. Joe then took time out to put my Dream Tan on and then I helped him to pump up. The atmosphere was fraught, all the guys there were looking good, their gaunt faces from the many months of dieting complementing their ripped up physiques.

Suddenly the call-out went for Joe's class. I wished him good luck and he stepped in line in one of the best groups of over-40s competitors I had ever seen. There were about 20 guys vying for the title and I knew that I had plenty of time, but unfortunately because the Dream Tan smears so easily I couldn't rest. I just took my time, took my Viagra and a swig of my red wine concoction and concentrated on what I had to do.

Other guys were prowling, driven by adrenaline, but I knew I had to relax so I just found a quiet spot far away from the others and let them try to psych each other out. I could hear the calls and the crowd shouting out their favourites. The noise seemed like an endless storm of whistles, screams and voices all mangled into one. The volume was rising and it was so tempting to start pumping up too early. I came back to the dressing room, took another drink of the red wine and started to ingest some chocolate.

I could feel the testosterone, the grunts of guys straining and gasping with the exertion of pumping up, then strutting to the mirror like a gorilla trying to impress a mate and hitting their best poses to try to intimidate the opposition.

I started slowly using my warm bands, concentrating hard on the muscles and seeing them bulge and fill with blood. I found some space and was just in the middle of doing some press-ups when they asked us to wait in line at the back of the curtain. I felt my throat go dry and had to take a sip of water. I realised that I was nervous despite all the years of competing. My adrenaline was pumping.

The call came to go on stage. We all stood in line and you could hear the guys breathing hard, tensing every sinew. Now and again someone would break out into a pose and the crowd would cheer and that would start a falling domino effect as adrenaline and nerves drove the other competitors to follow suit.

I was there in front of the judges, straining everything including the cheesy smile. We did the mandatories. Guys were streaked in sweat as they drove their bodies, that had been forced to survive on such little food for many weeks, into simple quarter turns. It does look simple to the crowd but you are working hard to create the illusion of simplicity, while inside you are trying to hide any weaknesses and emphasise the positives.

Guys were now panting with the effort as we were ordered to the back of the stage behind a two-foot platform to await our call-outs. I eagerly awaited my fate as I listened to the judges give the first call but my number wasn't one. I watched deflated as the athletes who had been chosen exhaustedly went through their comparisons.

In the next call I was selected but I had the two-foot barrier to get over and with my injury problems and the tiredness, this seemed like an obstacle in an Army recruitment test. I managed to get on top of it and then dropped over the platform. I landed like a brick, a dull thud accompanied me and I felt my dodgy back twinge as I stood in line. The lights seemed hotter than they ever have before. I felt drained, but I was determined, I ground out each pose, my body shaking with the effort. I could hear other people gasp and scream with the exertion. This was for the title and everybody was giving it everything they had.

I walked around the platform on my way back. There was no way that I was risking injury and just as I arrived back, I was called out again. Each time I stood in line with my peers and fought both the mental and physical pain as the lactic acid built up. I got three out of the five call-outs and although I was exhausted just like all the other guys, I was pumped full of adrenaline and I wasn't prepared to show any mercy to myself or my fellow competitors.

At the end of the final line-up we left the stage to thunderous applause. I saw Joe backstage and he helped me wipe some of the tan off my body. We both got dressed and gathered up our possessions. All we knew was that we had given every fibre of what we had to offer and the results would be announced that night.

Joe thought that I was in the top six, who get trophies and get to pose at the night show. I wasn't sure as I thought the problems with my digestive system had forced me to lose muscle and at this level, I knew I would had to have been at my best.

Jo and Joe's girlfriend, Wendy, were there to greet us. I felt emotionally exhausted. I had gone through so many different feelings: elation, fear, depression and anger had all visited me during the competition.

I sat there watching the rest of the show trying to eat some more flapjacks, but I was still feeling the usual sharp acidic pain that accompanied me when I tried to digest anything. The line-ups came out one after another but my mind wasn't there. I was responding to conversation but inside I felt like I had closed down and everything was surreal. It was only when we went out to the auditorium that I came to as though I had come out of a trance.

The guys were all saying that I was placed, they seemed upbeat, but I found it hard to raise a smile and winced as I ate a post-competition meal of cheeseburger and fries. I saw Sol from the supplement company that I had worked for, he had a stall there advertising his wares and he came across and started to talk to Joe and me.

He was his usual enthusiastic self and he sat with us and chatted non-stop about bodybuilding. Most of the conversation went over me like waves over a rock. All I wanted was to get back on stage and get the results. I don't know why but we had to vacate the premises while they set up the night show. It was with great reluctance and a lot of bloody persuading that I left my comfy seat and went outside the venue. I don't know what the population and visitors of Southport must have thought about the hordes of brightly-clothed bodybuilders, some of them still with their brown war paint etched on their bodies camped in little clusters outside the hall. It looked like an army had invaded the town and in a way, we were, we shared the commonalities of our sport and we were instantly recognisable to both one another and the outside world.

I remember having this nice dream that I was eating cheesecake when Jo woke me up to say that they were going back in again. I could see the masses of little camps of competitors and their followers suddenly coming to life.

The place was now sold out. It was filled wall-to-wall with people, the noise was unbelievable as people chatted and made their way to their seats. I said goodbye to Jo and Wendy as me and Joe left to take our places.

Backstage was a lot less hostile though, people now seemed more relaxed and even when the tanning booth made its second appearance, there was little complaint.

I helped Joe and then watched as he was called in line and then prepared myself. I knew that the results were in but I wanted to be seen at my best, so I began my pump-up. I could hear the fantastic roar of the crowd that saluted every pose of the over-40s guys. You could feel the vibes transmitted to all of us that were getting ready to do battle again. Guys that seemed totally knackered and weary suddenly seemed invigorated again.

I saw Joe come off stage with his British final medal. He hadn't made the top six but he seemed happy and as I passed him, I gave him the thumbs-up. I stepped on the stage with the other competitors to an amazing eruption of noise; people were screaming and shouting. My adrenaline started to flow and I was hitting poses like I had an abundance of energy. It was hard to keep still in the electric environment that the crowd had made.

We did the mandatories again and then the MC shouted "pose-down". I don't know where I got the energy from but Usain Bolt would have been proud of my five-metre sprint. I claimed the main stage point and the screaming drove me through a steady stream of poses. It was frenetic out there, people pushing, using their elbows to create more room to display their physique.

As the music died and the MC announced we should return to the back of the stage we all looked at each other, we all knew that it was over, years of training and dieting had brought us all to this moment in time and the next few minutes would see if all the sacrifices had been worth it.

It was like having a tooth extracted slowly as the final six places were announced in no particular order. Each time he said a new name my hopes would rise and then be dashed until finally the last of the six names was called out.

The tiredness suddenly hit me. I had given everything and I now felt like a punching bag that had been used by George Foreman in his heyday. I struggled with my clothing; I didn't want to leave the sanctuary of backstage to face the reality that I hadn't placed.

It was Jo who met me first, she just held me and kissed me. I don't think that she cared that I covered her in tan this time, she knew I was hurt and I needed her love at that moment.

People came up to me and said they thought I had placed, but in reality, the fact that I hadn't been able to carb up properly had really cost me. I had lost too much weight and much of it must have been muscle. The judges hadn't "robbed me" as my friends said, but whatever was causing this acid indigestion had.

I left the arena in despair and the ride home made me feel even worse; not even stopping at a local chippy and having my favourite pudding and chips helped. I struggled to eat it due to the indigestion and ended up leaving most of it. By the time we got home it was late, the night seemed silent and I was left alone with my thoughts as Jo slept silently beside me. The cupboards and fridge were safe that night, there was no late feasting, just me realising that I would have to get the indigestion problem sorted out but before I did I had the NAC Open British in the morning.

For the first time since I competed I slept right through the night, I didn't even wake up to go to the toilet, and in fact I think Jo had to wake me up about 10am. I didn't feel any excitement. I slowly got out of bed and tried to stretch my torso out and heard the familiar cracking of my back. I was greeted by the mirror as it reflected back a physique that was as waterlogged as a fourth division football pitch on a rainy winter evening.

I felt like Roberto Duran in his second fight with Sugar Ray Leonard, when he sat on his stool and stoically said: "No mas." I didn't know what had gone wrong and at this stage I knew there was no magic wand or drug that could rectify it.

I used the time before the show to relax and try to eat some nice food but digesting anything was still causing me so many problems that I had to use the bottle of indigestion medication so much that I wondered if you could overdose on Gaviscon.

I arrived at the venue around 2pm to sign in. I noticed that there were a few of the guys who had competed the day before with me. We seemed to be waiting an age before we could sign in and then I heard a girl laugh and some people were shouting. I looked outside and there coming across the car park, his huge physique dwarfing everything in sight, was Tony, Joe's mate. Scuttling in front of him on a lead was this tiny dog which, obviously because of its master's size, had developed some kind of delusional image about itself because it behaved and strutted like a heavily-muscled bulldog that growled menacingly at everyone.

I had to smile as I saw Tony pick it up in his massive arms that threatened to engulf the tiny hound. I just couldn't have imagined him with this ferocious little terrier; I thought he would have gone for at least a rottweiler or pit bull to match his tattoos and Mohawk haircut.

Spirits were fairly good backstage and the usual tension wasn't there. People were chilled and chatting to one another but I don't know if this was because we were all so completely knackered that we couldn't be bothered to psych each other out, or we knew one another that well and it wasn't worth trying.

When Joe from Silvers came backstage to get ready it felt like an eternity since we had started out on this journey at the North West just a few weeks before. I started to pump up and went through the procedure like I had done so many times before, but my body didn't feel like my muscles were swelling. It was like an out-of-body experience. I was giving it my all but nothing I did seemed to work.

I think we were all happy when they called us to get on stage. The line-up had five of the top guys in the sport and the crowd went wild as we were called out to do our comparisons. I was going at it toe to toe with the guys. I could hear someone grunting with the effort of striking yet another pose and I then realised it was me that was making the noise. I was called out for the second line-up. I stood there trying to keep tight but my body was betraying me, it was crumbling in front of a near capacity crowd, yet I couldn't flex the muscles and even the usual cheesy smile was now a painful grimace.

I could hear my friend John shout: "Keep tight Jim, be confident," but I couldn't take heed of his words.

I was called out in the next round and I could hear my friends getting behind me. My body was shaking as I tried to force out the appropriate poses. I could hear the other guys, they were hurting too, and everyone was breathing hard under the hot lights.

I was relieved that the sixth and final line-up didn't involve me so I just stood, my body now drooping. I made no effort to keep tight and my friends had long stopped shouting at me to do so.

I looked at the three guys in front of me as they strained once more and for the first time in my life I didn't give a damn where the judges had placed me, I just wanted to leave the stage and sit down somewhere.

The MC announced "pose-down" and I don't know if it was the dirty looks we all gave him or that he just saw five guys who were out on their feet, but a few seconds into it, as we all reluctantly went through the motions of trying to pose, I think they checked their insurance and decided that they weren't covered for five dead 50-year-old bodybuilders on their stage and they stopped the music. The MC announced to a startled audience that they thought we had been worked hard enough already as most of the guys had been competing yesterday.

It was just exhausting standing on the stage now. I was sad but relieved that they announced the placing quickly and I was given fourth place. It hit me as I trailed back with the other competitors that this was the end of the season for me; I had to sort this acid indigestion problem out and get back on track next season.

The dressing room felt a lonely place. It seemed strange, I had so many incredible nights where I had been hailed as the victor, but now I was bowing out on a season that had been one of my worst. I internalised whether it was my age. Had I had enough of competing? Was this the end? I didn't know anything as I walked back to Jo and my friends.

It was an uncomfortable meeting. They didn't know what to say to me and to be honest I didn't know what had gone wrong either. I said my goodbyes to the guys and got into the car for the short drive home.

Licking my wounds

I WAS tired, beaten, and I felt that I had let everyone down, including myself. I looked in the mirror and saw an old man staring back at me, but in my eyes I could still see that skinny guy who had the eye of the tiger. I smiled to myself. I knew I would be back and under my breath I said: "One more season, I can't bow out like this."

The next day I went into the chemist and asked for some medication for indigestion. The pharmacist asked about how it affected me and stated I really should see my doctor, but I foolishly ignored her and finally she suggested an over-the-counter medication called Ranitidine.

It worked wonders. I felt better within hours of taking it and I remembered my hero Tom Platz once saying after a competition where he had not placed: "Three days of eatin! Then training with brutal force."

This underpinned my plan to compete in May 2011. I could eat now without the pain and for the next three days I ate anything I wanted and didn't lift a weight. It felt fantastic, my whole body seemed to swell with muscle, it felt like someone was using a bicycle pump on me. Within the first three days I had put a stone of weight on and I looked full but still cut to ribbons.

It filled me with enthusiasm so I decided to use the "rebound growth" that you get when you start eating after months of dieting and used it with sustanon, trenblone and growth hormone.

The effects were amazing. I was as strong as ever in the gym, losing had not affected me and I was back to training like the underdog. I was hungry, very hungry.

I looked around the gym as I needed someone who was as intense as me, someone as strong, if not stronger than me. I then heard him. It was young Al screaming out the reps, his face a picture of self-loathing and desperation to complete his set. People stood around him, just watching with a mixture of admiration and horror at what they perceived as torture, but all I could see was maybe he could be the training partner I needed.

It was between John and Al because I knew it wouldn't just be good enough to train with intensity, it would have to be near insanity and who better than my two mates to fulfil that role? So dedicated or insane were my friends that they once found themselves training in the total dark when there was a power cut in Bury. It was one Saturday night after the gym had closed. They used to have the keys to the gym, and they were working up to five plates a side of squats when the lights went off. Anyone else would have called it a draw and gone home, but not Al or John, they trained on, utilising the faint lights of their mobile phones to grind out set after set.

I knew that John had just won the Universe, which is the ultimate prize in our sport, and that he was thinking about retirement. At that moment he was recuperating from nearly killing himself because he had decided to compete as a lightweight, which meant he had to drop over 14lbs of his already ripped-up frame. He was shredded alright, but in the weeks before the show he looked close to death and we were all questioning John's sanity. His face looked sunken to the point you could see the outline of his skull and he literally staggered from session to session and the odd grunt or nod was the closest he came to conversation.

Jo had seen him in the local precinct a week before his competition. At first she had passed John, because he was sat with a number of elderly folk and she had presumed it was a pensioners' outing because at the time he looked much older than 35 and apparently he had blended in so well with the rest of the group. It wasn't until the sprightly older group moved and left this "old chap", looking wizened and ill all alone, that she realised it was actually John!

I ended up training with Big Al as he was known by then. He had competed a few times and had really packed some muscle on. I never once thought that he was 30 years my junior, all I could see was someone as seriously addicted as me.

The workouts were heavy. Al liked the Dorian Yates approach and used one or two sets as a warm-up, then one all-out set that included negatives, which meant if you were doing bench press, he would help me when I was fatigued to push the bar and I would have to slowly lower the bar under control.

This was okay until I found out Al went to failure on everything including free squats which meant when he was totally fatigued, I would stand behind him and cradle him with my arms and assist him to stand back up on the final repetition. This was normal procedure for most people, but Al was different. I could feel his body straining and then crumbling under the weight of the squat as I helped him back up and in my mind I thought that's it, he has "repped out" which basically means he was exhausted and now I expected him to rack the bar.

But no not Al, he suddenly went down again. I nearly ended up catapulting over the top of him and then I felt his body go limp. He was spent but he wasn't giving in and my poor old back felt like it was as a mixture of his guts and my shocked, creaking body slowly hoisted the bar back into the squat racks.

Because of work and Al's commitments we could only train twice a week together, but each session was brutal and I looked forward to each session as it was hard to take yourself to the limit when training by yourself and people avoided training with me or Al.

Sometimes for a change we would go to a well-known gym in Rochdale. Its owner was a pro bodybuilder and the place had some really hardcore machines where we could hammer our backs. I would pick Al up on a Saturday and watch as he would squeeze into my car and manoeuvre his heavy frame into the seat. You could feel the car's suspension quaking as he got in. He may have been young, but he was as big and as strong as anyone I had seen and his dream was to one day be a top professional.

Al was training to compete at the UKBF North West at Warrington so our shows were close together and it would be good to do the cardio work as it used to bore me to hell.

It was January, I was over 16st and fairly lean, and I had feathers running down my quads because my condition was so good. I had started to clean my diet up after a good Christmas. Al was training and pushing me through the workouts. I still loved the regime but I was feeling my age and as the month wore on, despite giving everything I had, I felt like my body wasn't recovering. I would train Saturday and then have to rest all day, sometimes even staying in bed all the next day.

Al was like an express train that I was running alongside trying to catch, but each session I would turn up and give my all. It wasn't until February that I had to make my excuses. Al and I thought I just needed a few weeks of low-intensity work to get my body rejuvenated. I decided to have the week off and it did seem a lot better. I even looked forward to the Saturday to train with Al and as we trained, I was back on track. I was ripping the hell out of the workout.

The following day I told my brother I didn't know what was happening. Could it be the chronic fatigue? I actually said to him: "I feel like I am dying." These words would come back to haunt me a week later. On the Saturday, I turned up to train shoulders with Al and as the session got going, I could feel myself really getting into it. I was determined to blast myself out of the rut that I seemed to be in and we blitzed the workout, really smashed it, heavy and no mercy. I felt so good that I even joined Al on the bike for an hour's cardio.

Al commented that I was back to my old self and in truth I felt so good that I weighed myself and then we spent some time looking at my condition. I was 16st 5lbs and I was seriously cut, not in competition shape but about six weeks out, I knew I was on target for the NABBA North West.

I drove Al back home and we arranged to meet later in the week to train quads. I was feeling good as Saturdays were my day for having a cheat meal and tonight Jo had arranged for us to have our own Chinese feast. When I arrived home Jo was still out, so I snacked on some cooked pieces of chicken and watched some sport on the TV until she got back.

When Jo arrived home a few hours later, I could smell the distinct odour of barbeque spare ribs – my favourite – accompanying her as she came towards me and gave me a kiss. I helped her arrange the table with different dishes of ribs, spring rolls and fried rice that she had made herself. I couldn't wait to get tucked in, but after only a couple of mouthfuls, I could feel the now familiar acid reflux ripping through me. I instinctively reached for my last two Ranatidine tablets and swallowed them with milk.

I went to bed early that night because I began to feel rough and I remember waking up in the night and the acid pain felt like someone was stabbing me. It was a rough night for me and the bed sheets were evidence of this; they were saturated with sweat and strewn all over the place.

Nightmare in broad daylight

THE DAY I nearly died started off like many of my recent days had, crippling stomach pains and nausea, so it didn't seem anything out of the ordinary that I felt so tired I needed to stay in bed.

It was while I was watching football on the television; I think it was a friendly international against Brazil. I was alone, Jo had gone out with her mum and I got the feeling I wanted to be sick. Light-headiness greeted me as I stumbled into the bathroom, sure enough I was sick, but the sight that came to my blurred vision wasn't one of a sickly carrot colour, it was bright red and the realisation hit me, it was blood that I had just brought up.

A few paces and seconds later I was sick again. I tried to get to the sink but most of it cascaded down the sides and dripped in slow motion on to the carpet. For some reason and probably my obsessive compulsive nature, I didn't think "shit", I just thought I had better clean up the bathroom and I staggered into the kitchen to get a cleaning cloth that was housed in the cabinet under the sink.

I don't remember what happened in those few seconds or minutes, but I awoke to be facing the green of the kitchen wall and in my befuddled mind I thought I was still in bed watching the football.

I could feel myself shaking as I lay there and I knew that I had to get into bed. Those few yards were one of the toughest journeys that I ever made. I kept feeling as though I was going to black out again and I welcomed the safety of the edge of the bed and allowed myself to flop, exhausted and freezing with cold into its warm embrace. I started to come around a little and lifted the duvet up closer around my shoulders.

I could hear Jo's voice and realised that I had got through to her on the phone. Everything felt surreal but I knew that she was coming home and then I found myself talking to my brother as I just knew that I had to fight the urge to sleep. I told him what had happened. My voice sounded matter-of-fact as I described everything in detail. I could sense his urgency and he said that he wanted to phone an ambulance but for some reason it felt as though nothing needed that kind of drastic action.

Surprisingly when Jo got home, I was still calm, very matter-of-fact and got out of bed and met her at the door. I no longer felt dizzy but after talking to Jo, she helped me get dressed and she drove me to the accident and emergency department. I remember sauntering into reception and telling the clerk my name and address and that I had just vomited up blood about half an hour ago.

There were only a few people waiting and as usual even at this comparatively early time, there were signs of the "English disease" as people who were obviously worse for drink shouted and gesticulated about the time they had to wait. I don't think it helped the situation that almost immediately I was summoned in to see the triage nurse. She listened to me as I graphically detailed what had happened to me. She took my blood pressure and pulse rate and rather then returning me to the waiting room, she accompanied me to a cubicle and told me to lie down. I was left alone and the clinical-looking curtains were closed as she exited.

For a few brief moments I had the opportunity to try to fully grasp what had happened in what seemed such a short period of time. I closed my eyes and tried to relax and then it hit me, like some horrendous real life excerpt from *The Exorcist*. I could see in graphic, vivid detail pictures of me vomiting blood as though I was watching a film. It was interrupted by Jo's voice; she had parked the car and was now at my side. It felt comforting to have her hold my hand and as I smiled and looked at her, a doctor came in and introduced herself. I reiterated what had happened and she told me that they would need to put a cannula into my arm so that they could do blood tests to see if I was bleeding internally.

The next few hours were a blur. Blood tests came back okay and the worst part for me was that I had to have a rectal examination to also look for evidence of a bleed. As I lay there I began to think everything would be okay, I wanted to go home and when the doctor came back, I fully expected her to say that I was being discharged. My heart dropped when she said that they were going to keep me overnight for "observations".

The next thing I recall was that a wheelchair was brought to me and as you know from reading the earlier chapters in my book, wheelchairs and me are not good companions. I argued that I was okay and just wanted to go home, but Jo and the doctor insisted that I should stay. It was with great reluctance that I got into the chair and was wheeled to a near-deserted medical ward. The nurse documented me in and I was given some horrible green pyjamas to put on. I remember saying that I was going to keep my tracksuit bottoms on as I wasn't going to stay long.

It was at that moment that I felt sick again and rushed to the toilets a few feet in front of me. I felt dizzy and just about made it to a sink, where I vomited a small amount of blood. Jo eased me back into a commode which was parked nearby and went to get a nurse. As they arrived in the bathroom I projectile-vomited blood which I was told pebble-dashed the whiteness of the sink and walls. The last thing I remember was a nurse saying: "He looks terrible white; let's get him back to bed."

I don't remember passing out. I do know that I was having a nice dream about me and Jo being in the Lake District and then suddenly I was fighting with someone, I remember throwing punches at them, but they were holding me firm and I couldn't open my eyes. I was thinking that I had to get my eyes open and get away from them, I was struggling but they wouldn't let go. Open your eyes! Open your eyes!

I had to get away from this horrendous dream and then suddenly like I had been transported into a scene from hell itself, I was back in reality. The room resembled a scene from a battlefield.

There was blood everywhere, dark crimson blood, I could smell and see it and then I sensed many people, talking, pulling at me. My hands were being held and through blurred vision, I traced along my arms to see Jo's fingers tightly holding my hands and then I slowly looked for her face. She smiled, but in her eyes I could see fear. To me, her face represented a place of refuge in a sea of horrors.

Doctors and nurses were humming around me like bees in a nest. Some were putting lines into veins; so many that after their life-saving handiwork I resembled a marionette. Others were cleaning me up and cutting off the clothing that I had on and one doctor was preparing to give me a blood transfusion. I don't know if they put me on something to sedate me but in this maelstrom of activity, even though one poor startled patient was asking if I was dead, I was relatively calm. I was asking what had happened and whether it was a bleeding ulcer.

It felt reassuring when one doctor said that it was probably what had happened in her opinion, but that I would soon be going down to theatre to have an endoscopy so that they could find out. As I was transferred to a clean bed I became aware that apart from the green and blue uniformity of their clothing, most of the staff now had the addition of my blood on them. It was becoming clear that I had suffered a very severe blood loss.

I don't know how long we waited for the theatre staff that had been recalled to the hospital to arrive, but between Jo and the staff, who made jokes about having to change their uniform and how they were going to bill me for the dry cleaning, I was kept calm.

I knew things were bad as eventually I was taken down a long corridor. Jo was still holding my hand and her re-assuring smile was still rigidly in place, but with the now unfamiliar accompanying fear in her deep brown eyes. I could hear the anaesthetist introduce himself but all I could see was Jo. I wanted to tell her that I loved her more than life itself. She bent down and gave me a kiss and as she did so I said in my heart: "Goodbye my beautiful Jo."

As the trolley was wheeled on, I tried to see her. I knew that this time I was staring death in the face and now I was leaving the woman I loved and probably forever. Those few yards that I was pushed were the loneliest, most desperate ones of my life and I wasn't with any of the people who were close to me.

I wasn't anaesthetised fully, only sedated at first as they tried to push the telescopic tube down my throat. It felt as though I couldn't breathe and even though I was weak, I ripped it out. The staff tried to hold my hands down and the tube was inserted again and I heard the surgeon state: "His stomach is full of blood."

I couldn't breathe, probably through fear, but somehow I freed my hands and ripped it out again. I could hear the doctor saying that he would have to put me fully under. It seemed to be an age that I was lying there, but then I heard a voice that seemed from afar telling me that they were going to anaesthetise me and the next thing I knew was that an oxygen mask was being placed over my nose and I was told to breathe deeply.

In my mind I knew that death was near, I was staring down both barrels of the rifle and the safety was off, but I was so weak at this point that I welcomed the velvet arms of unconsciousness. My last thoughts were not from the bodybuilding bible, they were from a fearful human being fighting to stay alive. I fell out of consciousness, into the arms of Morpheus, thinking: "Fuck 21-inch arms, I need to fight like hell to keep alive."

I don't know how long I was out but Jo tells me that she spent the next few hours pacing nervously, making calls to her mum and my brother. I had the strangest dream when I was anaesthetised. I dreamed that I was talking to my old dad and he was telling me that I couldn't stay there because it wasn't my time.

The next thing I remember was that I was shaking, my body felt icy cold and I could hear a voice, faint at first like it was from somewhere in the distance. I could hear it clearer now, it was saying: "James, you need to calm down." I couldn't make out where it was coming from but there were hands, many hands, holding me down. I could feel my heart beating. I felt terrified. A myriad of thoughts erupted through my consciousness like a rocket exploding. Was this death? Was I dead? Where was I?

I don't know how long it took me to realise that the voice that I could hear wasn't the voice of God, but was one of a mortal being. I was so weak, my mouth felt as dry and as rough as sandpaper and bit by bit the realisation that I was alive and the theatre staff were trying to calm me drifted like a dark cloud as I became aware that this wasn't Heaven.

Far from it, my eyes now took in the stark, clinical place that had been the location where a handful of surgeons in green had fought for my life. I could hear another voice: "He went into tachycardia", as I felt what seemed to be a mountain of blankets loaded on to me. I could feel the weight as though it was pushing my body into whatever I was lying on. My arms seemed like they were shackled by chains as the bed started moving.

Everything seemed like a blur. I knew that Jo was with me, I don't know if I saw it or sensed it, but it felt comforting as I was loaded into an ambulance. I could feel the motion as it moved. I don't know how long it took but I slowly became aware of the whirling noise of the sirens and then I guess I must have been drifting in and out of consciousness because suddenly there was darkness and I could feel the cold night air on my face.

I could hear the feet of the ambulance men as they walked quickly and the next thing was that I was on a ward. It was dark, very quiet, like it was in the middle of the night. Nurses were threading drips into me but I could feel no pain, just the matter-of-fact tone of their voices as they talked to someone beside me and then I saw her face, it was my Jo, she kissed me tenderly on the cheek and through a hoarse, weak voice. I managed to whisper that I needed to pee and that I wanted a drink. I don't know if it was a male or female nurse that held my cock while I managed to wee into some kind of bottle, but I do know it must have been a difficult manoeuvre as I think through all the trauma, it had probably become inverted.

It was frightening lying there in the dark, with Jo sat there, looking as though she had been through the depths of hell. Beyond the surface smile that she tried to re-assure me with I could see the nightmare that she had to walk through with her eyes wide open. I could see that she was weary as I drifted and told her to go home. I was frightened that the rush hour traffic would soon be into full flow and that in the centre of Manchester, where I thought I was, it would take her hours to get home. I don't know what time she left me but it was still dark and I flitted into sleep for what seemed to be a few minutes, before being ripped back into reality by stark visions enveloped in crimson red, highlighting each and every detail of my living nightmare.

Time seemed to drag as though someone had placed a weight on the hands of the dials of the clock. I could hear the seconds slowly clicking away and then the long beeps of machines recording my vital signs above my head, intermittently blocked out by the whooshing sound of the automatic cuffs that were fixed around my arm that were used to take my blood pressure.

The ghostly white costume of a nurse came into my eye line and she looked directly above me, almost as if I didn't exist, and then she started to write something on the pad located at the bottom of my bed before seemingly floating away to the other patient next to me.

Slowly the night turned to early morning and the lights of the ward flickered on and I could hear the garbled voices of the medical staff as they swept through the room. I lay there surveying my body, riddled with tubes and my wrists bruised and encrusted with blood from the many cannulas that had been inserted.

I could see the room more clearly now. There were just a handful of beds and each one had an array of machines around it. It slowly dawned on me that I was in the High Dependency Unit.

The doctor came to my side; she told me that I couldn't have any drinks or food for the next 48 hours. She explained that I had a Mallory Weiss tear, but unfortunately for me, it had ruptured across an artery and I had lost a lot of blood which was why they had given me a transfusion. She told me that the surgeon had managed to stop the bleeding by inserting an endoclip around the tear, but they would have to monitor me for the next two days to see if it was successful.

My mouth felt like I had crossed the Sahara desert as I nodded my head to indicate to her that I had heard what she had said. A nurse arrived at that moment and she brought me what looked like several square looking lollipops, but unfortunately for me they weren't a treat, they were small sponges that had sticks attached to them. She informed that I was to take one of the sticks and dip it into the glass of water that she had placed near my side and then moisturise my lips.

I have never crossed the Sahara on foot, but I can imagine that if someone had and they had come across someone offering them a small, wet sponge that they would have torn the person's hand off and I was no different. I greedily pressed the sponge to my parched lips and let the drips cascade down my face.

I had felt weak many times in my life but this was my lowest moment. I was tired but couldn't sleep out of fear. I lay there almost motionless, the faint hum of the machines and the person next to me, their chest croaking with an almost inhuman rattle that seemed to accompany nearly every breath they took.

I must have eventually dropped off at some stage because I became aware of different voices and shuffling feet and then as though it was a magic trick, Jo and my brother Dave appeared.

I felt the first trace of a smile cross my face. It felt good to see them both and I could feel some strength returning as I tried but failed to sit up.

Dave met my gaze; he looked sad and tired as he stared at the heart monitor pads that were stuck to my chest because of my earlier heart problems and the oxygen line protruding from my nostrils.

I can't recall the conversation but all I know is that their voices weren't required; their mere presence was all that I needed.

As they left me I felt a mixture of emotions. I wanted to go home with them but I was imprisoned by the many lines and tubes that bound me to my life-preserving bed. I knew that this would be my place of abode for some time and I reflected how just two days before, Big Al had said that I was in "awesome shape".

The lights of the ward slowly dimmed to signal the onset of the night. I felt lonely as I thought how I longed to be cuddled up with Jo. I tried to turn on one side but it was impossible, I was trapped on my back like an upside-down turtle.

The night-time symphony started again. Machines bleeped, people snored, farted and rattled as I floated in and out of consciousness.

The first two days that I spent in the High Dependency Unit passed like a snail on cannabis. At times it all seemed surreal, like I was viewing scenes from the programme *Casualty*. On the third day, however, things were looking up; I was allowed both sips of water and a milky protein drink. Now it may seem ridiculous to you but to me that small bottle of protein was heaven. I was determined to make it last and nursed it like a baby taking its feed.

That was about the highlight of my stay on the HDU. I was gutted to leave there in a way. It had felt reassuring but also damn irritating to have the bleeping of the machines, making sure that I was okay, and as they wheeled me out of there I felt slightly anxious that the ward that I was going on wouldn't be as hi-tech and how would they know if I started to bleed again?

The corridors were quiet as the porter and nurse escorted me through a labyrinth of dull white walls until at last, we arrived in a dimly-lit, long rectangular room and another nurse who I came to know as Sheila showed us to a unit that was to become my new home for days to come.

As I looked outside the window the outline of shadowy buildings looked almost ghostly. A random thought passed through my mind and stayed like someone had hit the brakes. I don't know why but I kept recalling the series *Life on Mars* where a woman after major trauma finds herself catapulted back in time to the 1970s. I glimpsed at the ceiling tiles above me as the low glow of the floor lights that had been switched on seemed to stop in mid-air. I couldn't get the stupid idea out of my head that somehow this was a sort of purgatory and that I had died, because no one could have lived through such a massive bleed as that.

I lay there, still anchored to the bed by the remaining drips and tubes, and internally chuckled. It was the first time in days that I had been able to raise a smile and as a deadly hush fell across the room, I allowed my body to surrender to the serenity and I fell into a deep sleep.

The next morning the consultant that had saved my life came to see me and the first question that he asked me was how much alcohol did I drink. I told him that I was virtually teetotal. He went on to explain that alcoholism and bulimia or any illness that caused people to retch or vomit frequently were strongly associated with it. He asked me if I took steroids as my body, because of the trauma and forced dieting, was ripped. My exposed arms were a mass of veins that resembled knotted spaghetti. I was open and honest with him and told him everything that I had used including something I hadn't really ever regarded as any real threat to my health: diclofenac.

As soon as I mentioned that I used the drug to counteract my rotator cuff and back problems I could see him nod. He told me that they may never find what actually the catalyst was but it was certainly feasible that diclofenac had something to do with it.

When he left me I was stunned. I knew that diclofenac could cause some people to have stomach bleeds, but no one ever mentioned it could nearly make you bleed to death.

It would be four more days before I was allowed home and in that time I had so many hours to ruminate. The past week had been hell. It had taken so much out of me and Jo both mentally and physically. It felt lonely lying there and my mind was like a washing machine filled with crumpled-up thoughts.

From somewhere I found myself contemplating retiring from competing only for it to be blasted away. As the low lights signalling night time came on I couldn't sleep, things kept revolving around my mind. I didn't want to quit. I had done it before, I had beaten the odds, but somehow as I lay there this felt different, there was a voice in my head that wouldn't go away.

It was saying this had to be the end. I tried to override it and rationalised that even when the chronic fatigue had been so acute, except for some really low periods, something deep inside had always driven me on and maybe I could rise from the ashes once again. But now as the night dragged on, all I could think about was how close I had come to dying and how I never wanted to experience that living nightmare again.

I had to complete two tasks before I would be allowed to go home and the first was to eat a "soft meal" of potatoes and ground mince. I was starving but bloody nervous of passing anything down the area that had been lacerated. They gave me a small teaspoon to eat it with and by the time I had finished by "licking" the plate, it was visiting time.

My second task was to use the toilet and take a dump, which if you have been in hospital, you will know isn't as easy as it sounds, especially when you have had so many different chemicals pumped into you.

When I finally did go it was the blackest-looking stool that I had ever passed, but it was also my ticket home.

I left the hospital the following day, escorted once again by "Sergeant Major" Jo and my brother. She held me under the arm and frog-marched me to the car and when we arrived home, I was unceremoniously marched into our flat and straight into a bed that she had prepared for me.

I uttered the formal protests that we men make in such circumstances, but to be honest I needed the rest. The small journey from the hospital had exhausted me.

Jo switched on the TV set and I melted into my bed. It was good to be home and it wasn't until I heard the rattle of bottles being put on my bedside that I realised that I must have fallen asleep. Jo was prompting me to take some tablets that she had in her hand and then I made the connection that this was the medication I would have to take to try to prevent another tear.

I was feeling relaxed and drifting to the point where you are being drawn into the a deep vacuum of sleep. It felt luxurious to be able to lie in my own bed. I looked at Jo, she was sleeping, lying contently with her head resting on my chest.

I don't know at what time I nodded off but I woke up early and stumbled in dark until I reached the bathroom. I groped for the light cord and yanked it and I was greeted by the stark vision that filled the room, and flashed out images that transported me right back to the scene of the hospital.

I could see myself vomiting thick clumps of blood. It looked so vibrant, so real that I had to touch the sink to see if it was really existed. I could see the drops of blood plopping onto the floor and creating a crimson puddle. My body shook as my mind was catapulted back in time. I could feel my body shaking as though someone had turned the room into a walk-in fridge. I was breathing like I had just finished a marathon, my legs felt weak as I lowered myself down onto the floor and sat, with my arms curled around me, trying to reassure myself that it wasn't real.

It was about 30 minutes before I had summoned up enough strength to get back to my feet and nervously made my way back to bed. Jo was fast asleep, softly breathing as I got under the covers. I lay there all night, shivering, freezing cold, but too alert with anxiety to go to sleep.

That was the first of many such episodes. It was like I was caught up in a never-ending replay. My mind seemed to act like a projector and graphically shot out images of me lying in the room bleeding to death.

I didn't know what was wrong. I had worked in mental health for years but now I felt vulnerable, like a surfer waiting to be wiped out. I never knew when it was going to hit me but when it did, it stopped me in my tracks.

I hoped it would go away. I was an Iron Warrior, these things didn't happen to me, but time after time the traumatic scenes revisited me and then the after-effects of severe anxiety would be with me all day and night. I would drift off to sleep, only to wake what seemed a few minutes later, breathless, shivering and freezing cold.

I truly thought that I was going insane. I was sleep-deprived and at first couldn't face my doctor because I didn't want to admit that I was experiencing some kind of mental health problems.

Jo eventually persuaded me to go and see my GP and it was with great reluctance on my part that I finally went to see her. She diagnosed that I was suffering some kind of post-traumatic problem and also depression so she gave me a prescription for diazepam and mirtazapine and made a referral for me to see a psychiatrist.

I felt at my lowest ebb. I knew both medications well because many of my clients were on them and this just confirmed to me that I was ill, not just physically but mentally too.

Weeks went by; I was avoiding going out and any contact with anyone but my brother and Jo. I was depressed, I wouldn't eat unless Jo stood watching me and then it would just be a token effort. I kept thinking: "Is this my life now?" I had fought through so many physical problems, but now

I was fighting something that wasn't real, it only existed in my mind, so how the fuck could I beat it?

The world seemed a bleak place, the depression and flashbacks attacked me at will. I was a defenceless target as their "claws" ripped me open minute after excruciating minute.

It was during some of these times that I contemplated ending it, I was in that much mental pain. There seemed no sanctuary and to my mind I couldn't live if I had to live like some of the people that I cared for who had mental health problems.

I don't know what kept me from doing it. I think it was more like a cry for help, but at the time it felt real. Getting through those months was tougher than getting in shape for any show.

I had to hold on to shreds of what I used to be and it wasn't until I saw a psychiatrist that I could get any understanding of what had happened to me. He called it post-traumatic stress and added as though it was an afterthought that I also, in his opinion, had been through some kind of "adjustment disorder" and my neurotransmitters, which are electrical impulses in the brain that regulate emotions such as anxiety, stress and pleasure, would take time to recover.

To you and me that meant that because I had been in a life or death situation, the resulting trauma and adjustment syndrome was apparently the brain's struggle to make sense of a sudden life change and this would often result in depression or anxiety.

It slowly filtered into my befuddled mind what was happening to me. I was facing a life away from competing. Since the age of about 14 I had been training and focused on preparing for events, not just at bodybuilding, but at running and other sports.

Now I was facing my nemesis, a dark place to which I had never wanted to go. Time after time I had seen other sportsmen retire and now I couldn't hide away from the fact that I was possibly facing that reality too. It hadn't been on a conscious level, but somewhere deep inside I think I had known my days were numbered, and that I probably couldn't get back to the high degree of fitness that competing at national level demanded.

Coaches train you physically and mentally for everything, but very few of them prepare the athletes for the massive adjustment to life without the thrill of competition, because that would be viewed as a negative and the whole ethos of training is focusing on the positives.

One moment you are on people's minds, on the stage enjoying the applause, the next you are absolutely alone. It is a place many well-known sportsmen and women have found themselves unceremoniously dumped.

I was lucky. For some people it wasn't just their sport, it was their livelihood too, not only do they have to retire but they have to find a new way of putting food on the table. It isn't really talked about because people brush it under the carpet. We can all understand our heroes having physical problems, but mental health ones are viewed, including by the athletes themselves, as an unacceptable weakness.

I had spent my years dividing my days into six to eight meals and different body parts, but I had forgotten there was a life before this had existed.

I knew deep down that I had to reinvent myself. I had to learn once more to be a human being. There was a time when I spat that word out with disgust too as any competitor who takes him or herself to the top of their sport has long since given up the privilege of a human being. You become a machine that is able to push yourself through pain, injury and adversity to reach your goal. This is what you live for, you mark time into sessions, food becomes a fuel source and not something to enjoy and when the competition days come to an end you grieve for them because despite all the pain and sacrifice, it's what you live for.

Seeing the psychiatrist made me feel slightly better as at least now I realised that there seemed a logical reason why I was experiencing these difficulties and I could start to try to make some sense of what was happening to me, but I still had to deal with the days when I felt like a bag of shite.

Sometimes I wouldn't shave or wash for days; I secluded myself away from everything including my family and friends. I felt so ashamed of what was happening to me. I was supposed to be the guy who had fought through anything. People revered me, some put on me on a pedestal and now at times I felt that I wasn't just falling off it, I was crashing to the floor into a thousand pieces.

It was around September that I had to return for an endoscope at Bury Hospital to analyse the laceration internally. It isn't a pleasant experience; they pass a camera down your throat. It feels like a thick corded rope as it passes down and your gag reflexes go on overtime. I lay there on my side, fighting the urge to rip the damn thing out of my mouth while the doctor positioned the camera and made his observations.

I saw the consultant later that same day and he imparted the good news that the laceration had healed, but I had a small hiatus hernia and he hypothesised that this may well have been the cause, but they had no definitive answers for me. He also advised me that I could train but not to lift heavy weights as some Mallory Weiss tears are caused by internal pressure brought about by the heavy lifting.

I left the hospital with mixed feelings; I knew that if I tried to return to heavy training, I risked another bleed. Back in my "immortal years" when I was younger and never contemplated if I would wake up the next morning, I would have gone for it. Now, however, I felt different, my recent close shave with death and being in my 50s had made me realise that I didn't have a fetish for wearing my undies over my trousers, nor did I own a cape and I definitely wasn't allergic to Kryptonite either and there would come a day when I would meet the Grim Reaper in person.

It wasn't so much the physical side of life that I was struggling with though. It was the flashbacks, and although they were abating they still ripped through me from time to time.

At least I wasn't starving myself now, but I was comfort-eating and everything that I could find, including Jo's uneaten Easter eggs, I devoured. It was hard to resist junk food. I had spent so many years eating clean and when I was on my own, I would find myself just eating out of sheer boredom.

I felt like a fake as I typed a reply on the bodybuilding forum that I write on with my avatar displaying this ripped, muscular physique. I felt far from that now. I tried to avoid looking at my body, but sometimes I caught a glimpse of it when I was getting dressed. It looked fat and my pecs that had once looked so hard and muscular now appeared soft and flabby and this compounded how I felt about myself.

I knew now that I could go to the gym and have a normal training session, my body would be okay if I just took it easy, but I had been conditioned to pushing myself to the limit year after year and I knew trying to adapt to a new way of training wouldn't be easy. But it was my mind that was now keeping me away. Apart from the flashbacks I was depressed, I was still grieving for the competitive years.

It was January 2012 and it was an extremely cold day when I finally got myself together and set out for the gym. I nervously paced outside, thinking that I didn't want people to see me like this and then I saw big Caz, a friend of mine. He just smiled and said "hi" as though he had seen me the day before.

I walked upstairs with him into reception and greeted some of the guys I knew only by sight. The place hadn't changed one bit. I don't know what I expected but as I sat down on the bench press, I smiled because I knew that I was "home". I may not be an Iron Warrior any more but I was still me. My thoughts were interrupted by John shouting: "Hey you old bastard, you feeling better now?" It was good to be back. I nodded to him and started pressing out the "baby weights" that I had loaded on the bar.

I guess that session was the beginning of my new life. I got to see a cognitive behavioural therapist soon after and she helped me to learn more ways of coping with the anxiety and depression. I also started a graded return to work, which meant that I was supposed to be working just a few hours a day, with less stressful clients. Although in my line of work it's often more like you're thrown back into the deep end.

The first day started with a call to an elderly chap called Mark, who lives in a warden-controlled property. He didn't answer when I rang his intercom which was unusual for him, so I ended up going up to his flat and after knocking and shouting for him to answer the door for about ten minutes, I contacted the warden to get in with the pass key. I could see in her eyes that she suspected the worst as we entered his flat.

There was an eerie silence that was suddenly broken by the warden shouting out to him, but no reply came. His bedroom door loomed in front of us and I knocked hard and called out to him once again, but still there was no reply. I opened the door and there he lay motionless and I looked at the warden with a degree of apprehension. It didn't look good.

Both the room and his body felt like ice as I tried to shake him, but he showed no signs of life. I couldn't even detect any breathing and then I leant over him and placed my fingers near his neck to try to locate a pulse, when suddenly, he leapt up into a sitting position, looking like a startled rabbit and said: "What's happening?"

At the same time I heard the warden scream like she had just witnessed a dead body coming to life. All I could think was: "Fuck me! A stress-free, graded return, my arse it is!" as I shook my head in disbelief at the Lazarus-style awakening of Mark.

My days of performing on the stage are over. I had always thought that there would come a time when the eye of the tiger would die inside me and that I would wake one morning and not want to train, but I guess it seldom happens like that in athletes. Most of us would love to be out there in the cauldron of competition so it isn't the desire that goes, it's the ability to be able to perform at the level that you used to that finally deserts you,

Competing at bodybuilding is like riding an express train. It is okay when you are on board, hurtling at break-neck speed, but if you get off for any reason, you have to work twice as hard to get back on and I have spent many years as that guy you see at the train station, rushing like the wind, making a last, desperate lunge to board the train as it was leaving.

Playing catch-up because of illness had become an occupational hazard to me but somehow in those dark moments in the hospital when all I could see was my body corded by life-saving tubes, deep down I knew that my time had come to an end.

When I started my first draft of the book I excluded the fact that I had taken performance-enhancing drugs, because I wanted to focus on just how tough the athletes have to be to take their mind and bodies through the endless years of hardcore training and cardio while existing for many weeks at a time on a diet that is almost inhumane, let alone try to have a working and family life as well.

In the end though I felt that I had to include their use. Not to endorse them, it would be totally wrong to do that, but because I have spent years reading so-called factual biographies that deny what they did to achieve their massive physiques and at the end of it, I thought what a load of bullshit.

Some people wanted me to write that I condemn drugs in sport and in a lot of ways I do, but then how can I take the moral high ground and lecture you, the reader? All I can be is honest and tell you the good, the bad and the downright ugly and let you guys make up your own mind.

People will always find something to give them an edge. We have to accept that the world doesn't come to watch the mediocre: it wants bigger, stronger and faster and the mega bucks are there for the taking if an athlete is the best at what he or she does. Our sport, unlike many, does not make the pretence that all our sportsmen are clean; it gives people a choice between tested and untested shows. I assure you that I am not looking at my sport through rose-tinted glasses. It has many pitfalls and I have fallen into lots of them.

It's time to leave you now. I hope you enjoyed the journey half as much as I did, but I would just like to say that although the flashbacks and chronic fatigue are still with me, I will always train and be involved in the sport of bodybuilding. I still try to hit the gym three times a week and sometimes I train with my old mate Kevin Alder. We no longer "beast" the workouts, but we don't mess around either and we still try to out-do each other. However the guttural screams of intensity have now been replaced by the sound of grinding joints and grunts of arthritic pain.

In any other sport, with the exception of golf or darts, I would have been finished long ago, but our sport promises longevity and health if it is done right. My advice to anyone starting out would be to look at our sport as a marathon, rather than a sprint. It is truly amazing to watch people who you can see queuing up for their pensions outside the Post Office on a Monday morning, strutting their stuff on stage at the weekend, looking healthy, muscular and ripped and without a zimmer frame in sight.

But you know what they say? "Bodybuilders never die – they simply lose their pump."